Creating Decorative Paper

Creating
Decorative
Paper

Paula Guhin

STACKPOLE
BOOKS

Published by
STACKPOLE BOOKS
5067 Ritter Road
Mechanicsburg, PA 17055
www.stackpolebooks.com

Printed in the United States of America

10 9 8 7 6 5 4 3 2 1

First edition

Cover design by Tessa Sweigert

Library of Congress Cataloging-in-Publication Data

Guhin, Paula.
     Creating decorative paper / Paula Guhin. — 1st ed.
         p.   cm.
     ISBN 978-0-8117-3646-6
     1. Paper work.   2. Decorative paper.   I. Title.
TT870.G84 2012
745.592—dc23
                                                                        2011032785

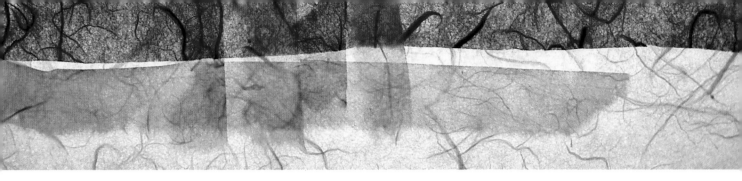

Contents

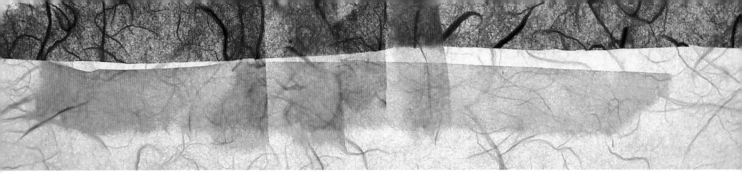

Acknowledgments

For his unflagging encouragement and assistance, I am extremely grateful to my husband, my cohort, and my accomplice in life. Thank you, David.

And thanks with all my heart to the gifted crew at Stackpole Books. Mark Allison, you are the best, and Kathryn Fulton, you have my gratitude.

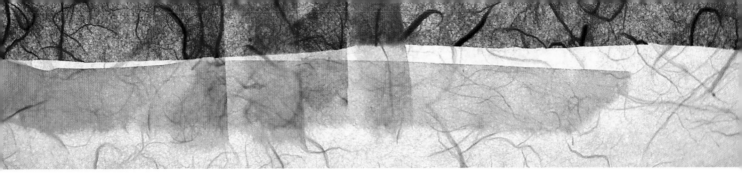

Introduction

Transform ordinary paper into an enchanting surface and employ it in any number of ways!

While an infinite variety of ready-made paper exists for the consumer, luscious papers decorated with your own hands can be customized to fit a particular theme, motif, and color scheme. You choose the techniques and materials, and you have the satisfaction of using truly unique papers. Original patterns and designs are the perfect starting point for any creation, be it gift wrap, place cards, name tags, a photo mat, or any other inventive project.

The techniques in this book are for play and exploration by anyone, regardless of perceived "skills." Experiment with the many possibilities of paints, inks, glues, and papers. Have a grand adventure with rich color, texture, imagery, and more. Try resists, layering, rubbings, faux finishes, and many more madcap approaches. And do it all with ease! The methods and designs within are simple, fast, and inexpensive to implement. (For that reason, I do not include commercial rubber stamping or embossing, topics covered well in many other books.)

Discover how to create scores of exciting effects with a wide variety of tools and techniques. Find fabulous projects with step-by-step, illustrated directions. Fire your creative spirit with inspiration!

Helpful tip boxes are scattered throughout this book. "Tip Talk" offers artistic advice, "Smart Swap" suggests alternative materials or tools, and "Going Green" presents eco-friendly ideas. The back matter includes a useful glossary meant to clarify visual art terms, and a resources list as well.

As always, be careful when handling art materials and tools. I recommend wearing rubber gloves and protective clothing. Precautions must be taken to avoid accidental ingestion, inhalation, and skin and eye contact. Be sure to keep containers closed and away from children.

This has been the most fun book I've ever written. Now let *your* enjoyable exploration begin.

CHAPTER 1

Papers, Paints, and More

You can add color and designs to all kinds of gorgeous
art papers—from rice and lace papers to parchment,
printmaking papers, even vivid cardstock.

Art Papers

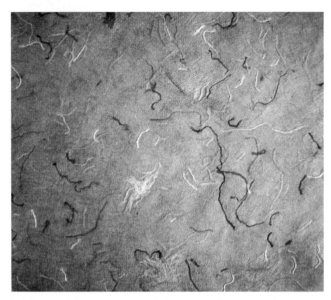

It is important to select the right papers for any project. Drawing, printmaking, and painting papers abound, from pastel and watercolor sheets to acrylic and others. Another category of art papers is the spectacular sort: dazzling, distinctive papers that are beautiful in their own right. The extensive art paper inventory on these pages may stir your creative muse into action! (Later we will discuss *other* types of surfaces on which to work.)

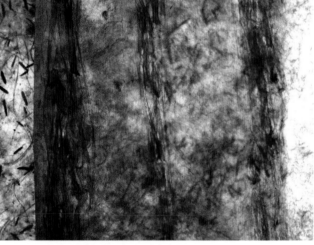

Some art papers contain leaves, bark, grasses, and other fibers. Allow their beauty to show through.

An assortment of Joss papers.

Ogura lace papers are strong, yet beautiful. These have been painted.

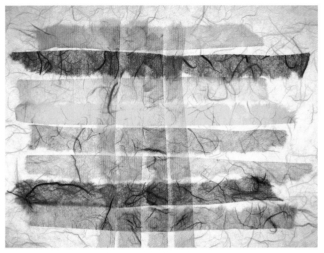

Mulberry papers can be purchased at scrapbook or art supply stores.

Made by hand, large sheets of printed art papers like these can be pricey.

Other Papers

Inkjet and copier papers exist in a rainbow of hues.

MORE ART PAPERS

Bleedproof paper for pens	Mulberry papers
Block-printed papers	Origami papers
Calligraphic papers	Papyrus and Thai papers
Canvas papers	Parchment papers
Cardstock	Pastel papers
Charcoal papers	Rice papers
Embossed papers	Scrapbooking papers
Fabric papers	Screen-printed papers
Japanese papers	Tracing papers
Marbled papers	Vellum
Metallic leafing sheets	Velour paper

This collage is a sampler of many found papers, including corrugated cardboard, brown Braille paper, and more.

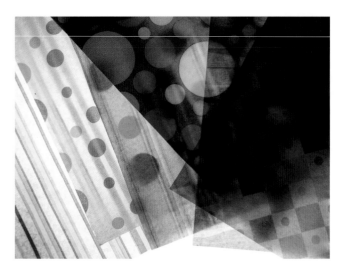

Commercially available gift tissue is both plentiful and useful.

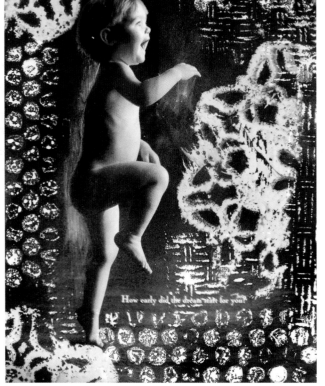

This magazine page was texture-stamped with found objects using acrylics.

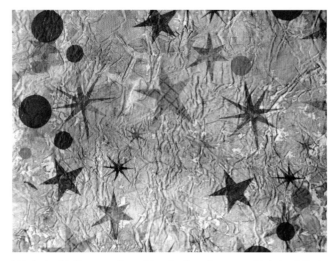

Printed gift tissue adhered to vinyl wallpaper which had first been painted with turquoise acrylic to enhance the texture.

A thin coat of gesso pales and partially obscures this comic strip.

Printed paper napkins with white or light backgrounds are far more translucent than darker ones.

TIP TALK

Keep all those types of paper organized! Stack similar colors together in a large, shallow box or gigantic ziplock bag. For instance, put gray or metallic sheets with beige, tan, cream, and brown. You can store all warm colors separate from cool colors, or keep printed and patterned papers separate from solids. Sort your stash in a way that makes sense to you.

EVEN MORE PAPERS!

Blotting paper	Homework pages
Blueprints	Kraft paper
Bogus paper	Ledger paper
Bond paper	Letterhead paper
Calendar pages	Mail order catalogs
Comic book pages	Manila papers
Computer printouts	Maps
Construction paper	Newspapers and newsprint
Cork paper	Old letters
Crepe paper	Paper grocery bags
Deli paper	Photocopies
Diagrams	Sandpaper
Dictionary pages	Scribbled, doodled-on paper
Dress patterns	Sheet music
Freezer paper	Tissue
Gift wrap	Vintage book pages
Graph paper	Wallpapers
Hand-drawn sketches	Waxed paper

Paints

I include pastels here, since pastel artists consider them to be traditional "painting" media. And while gesso is not technically paint, many artists use it as such, often as a wash. Besides the traditional white gesso, it also comes in black, clear, and other colors. You can even buy gesso spray in a can!

- Acrylic paints and mediums
- Gesso
- Gouache
- House paint
- Oil paints and mediums
- Oil pastels
- Soft chalk pastels
- Spray paint
- Tempera paints
- Watercolor paints

Pastel pencils or Contè pencils can be used to create rich, vivid papers.

Acrylic Paints

Acrylic paints come in many forms. They are water-based, although permanent when cured. Heavy body paint is thicker, and fluid paint is a liquid. Read more about acrylic inks on page 12.

Acrylics mixed with water can be used as watercolors.

Sheer acrylic washes enhance vintage sheet music.

There are many other acrylic mediums and additives, including various types of crackle paints and mediums. The acrylic polymer mediums most commonly used are liquid medium (gloss or matte—both are pourable) and gel medium, which is offered in various consistencies and finishes. Soft gel is thinner than regular gel, and heavy (or extra-heavy) gel is even thicker than the regular formula. Both fluid and gel mediums are adhesive. You can use them to change not only the consistency, sheen, or transparency of acrylic paint, but also some of the properties of paper. Most acrylic mediums that look white in the jar actually dry clear.

This page from an old architecture book was enhanced with paint and resin sand texture gel.

Explore the world of texture gels—specialty mediums with such additives as pumice, sand, glass beads, fibers, and more. Try them alone on heavy colored paper or mix them with paint. Here, pearl and gold mica flake and black lava acrylic gel on a gold-painted background.

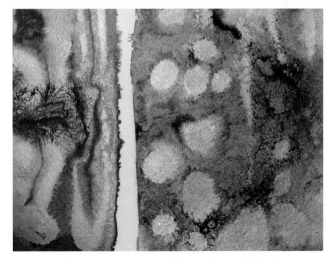

Gold and silver copper paint additives (also called effect mediums) were dropped into wet drawing inks in these examples.

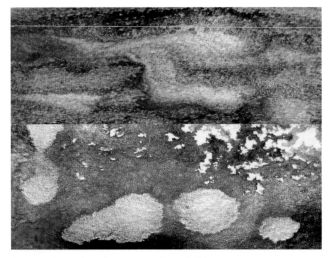

Dropped pearl and copper paint additives.

Markal Paintstiks by Shiva are convenient and easy-to-use oil-based paints.

Oil Paints

Traditionally, oil paints are thinned with solvents such as turpentine, which is flammable, carcinogenic, and has a strong odor. Traditional oil paints are extremely slow-drying, especially if you apply them heavily. The long drying time allows you to mix the colors with very subtle blending.

There are also water-mixable oils, however, that handle like conventional oils but thin and clean up with water. Another bonus: They dry rapidly.

Scraping a design with beautiful metallic oils.

Pastels

Oil pastels come in stick form and in many vivid colors. The best quality oil pastels are soft and creamy, not too waxy.

Oil pastels resist watercolor paint, diluted tempera, and gouache splendidly. Chapter eight will explore some of the resist effects you can produce with these.

Water-soluble oil pastels dissolve somewhat when washed over with water. The result can be similar to watercolor. Draw with them on dry or damp papers.

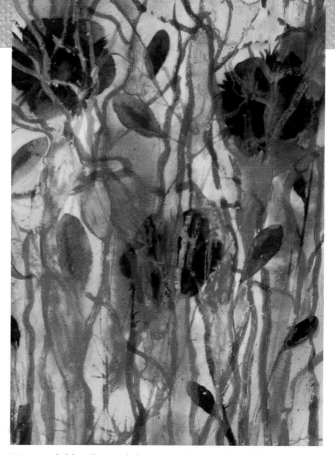

Water-soluble oil pastels have made a considerable change to the original inkjet photo.

This digitized watercolor painting was printed on glossy inkjet photo paper.

A second printout (on watercolor paper this time) was altered with water and water-based colored pencils.

Soft pastels, sometimes called chalk pastels, are available in several forms and grades. The best ones are buttery, intense, and easily smudged. Spray the finished page with fixative to preserve soft pastel on paper. Use aerosols only in a well-ventilated area.

You can create a smoother soft pastel painting by stroking over it with a wet brush.

Textured yellow pastel paper shows through in places owing to the graininess of the medium.

Paintable, textured wallpaper has raised areas that grab pastels nicely.

Watercolor Paints

Watercolors come in many forms, including tubes, semimoist pans and half-pans, cakes, and liquid form. Liquid watercolors are especially brilliant because they have high pigment content. The quality varies considerably depending on the brand.

The transparency of most watercolors lends a luminous quality to a painting; they are not meant to be used opaquely. Gouache and tempera, on the other hand, contain fillers that give them better coverage. Both gouache and tempera paint are matte and water-soluble when dry. Gouache is sometimes known as an opaque watercolor. It has also been called "designer's color" because of its use by commercial artists. Elementary students today customarily paint with tempera, or poster paint.

Watercolor markers, water-soluble pencils, and water-based crayons are also available.

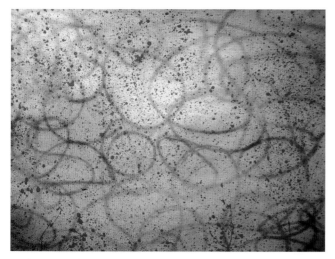

In this example, water-based markers were scribbled onto wet watercolor paper first. After it was dry, the paper was spattered for additional interest.

Inks

Liquid inks can be pigment- or dye-based, and transparent or opaque. They include India inks, colored drawing inks, and many more. Thicker, pastelike ink (such as printing ink) is another convenient medium worthy of exploration.

And don't forget permanent markers! Broad, extra-large, fine, and ultra-fine tips make for a wide range of exciting marks. Vibrant designer markers were used here on water-color paper.

Spray-on Water-based Inks

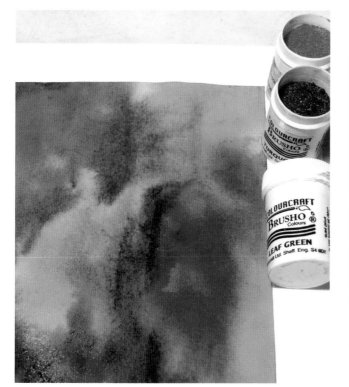

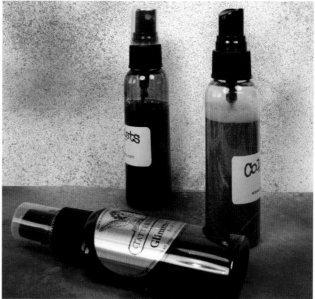

Non-aerosol spray watercolors such as Glimmer Mist or Smooch Spritz can produce beautiful effects, and the shimmery mists are especially stunning.

Some do not work well on glossy paper—they pool or bead up. Sometimes it's difficult to get an even mist, and large, unwanted droplets will appear. The nozzle clogs occasionally. Shake them well before using.

Colourcraft's Brusho inks are non-toxic and come in powdered form. When mixed with a small amount of water, they are transparent, very concentrated, and highly pigmented.

You can make your own metallic or pearlized watercolor sprays by mixing gum arabic and mica powder (PearlEx, Perfect Pearls, or other shimmery pigment powder) into a mini-mister filled with water. The amount of pigment powder is a matter of preference. Start with ⅛ teaspoon. Try the same amount of gum arabic. Shake well. Adding a few drops from a small bottle of reinking dye for stamp pads will alter the color.

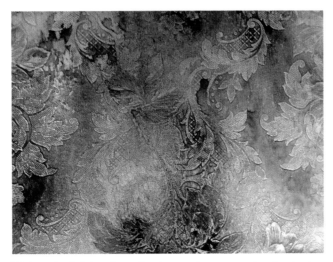

Watercolor ink beads up in places when sprayed onto vinyl wallpaper.

Alcohol Inks

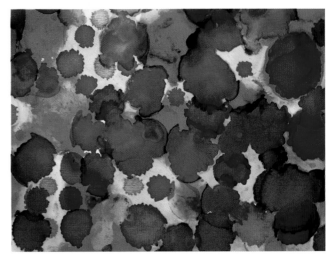

Alcohol inks are dye-based, transparent, and permanent; they will stain the hands, so wear rubber gloves when using them. Dilute them with alcohol-ink blending solution or rubbing alcohol. Since they absorb into soft, non-slick papers immediately, try them with hard papers like vellum or on glossy papers as shown here.

Felt applicator pads are optional but useful for blending. Another accessory, a fillable pen, is made especially for alcohol inks.

Acrylic Inks

Water-based (but permanent and water-resistant when cured) liquid acrylics dry quickly. They are available in both transparent and opaque versions.

Shellac-based Inks

These waterproof inks dry to a permanent sateen finish. Colors are blendable and can be reduced with a shellac-based thinner. They have a high degree of water resistance without being indelible.

Walnut Inks

These versatile products can be purchased as liquids or crystals. The latter can be dissolved (approximately one part crystals to four parts warm water). Try walnut inks with a variety of papers.

Walnut inks can enhance a watercolor or oil pastel painting, and they also work well with watercolor crayons. In this example, gold acrylic underpainting sets off walnut ink nicely.

Spray-on walnut inks come in many colors.

Sprinkling brown walnut crystals into small puddles of water adds distressed-looking dark areas. Note the lighter spots, made with liquid laundry bleach. Read more about bleaching in chapter 9.

A bit of pastel acrylic paint was used to enhance a few areas when the walnut ink was dry. Another option would have been to apply soft chalk pastel in places.

 GOING GREEN

Stained tablecloths, old shower curtains, and worn bedsheets can serve as dropcloths in the art studio.

Other Pigments and Dyes

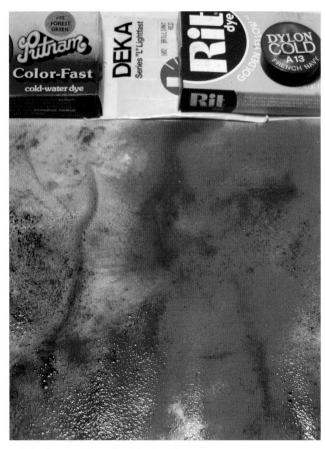

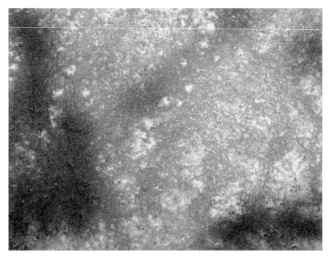

Dark teas and other natural dyes also will stain paper. Brew a strong, dark mixture or use wet tea leaves. Leave the latter on absorbent paper overnight for best results.

This watercolor paper was dampened thoroughly and stained with tea leaves.

Fabric dyes work well with absorbent papers. Some commercial fabric dyes are quite granular, although Procion dyes are finely powdered. They make a very strong ink when mixed with a little water.

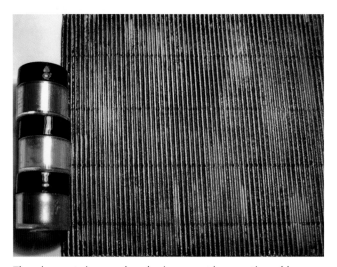

Finally, although this book doesn't include store-bought rubber stamps, we'll mention reinkers in this section. They're available in a huge assortment of colors and are meant for reinking stamp pads. Investigate their potential for surface decoration. They will stain hands, so wear rubber gloves.

The pigments in powdered micas must be mentioned here as well. The black corrugated paper used here shows off lustrous PearlEx powders.

TIP TALK

Use acid-free products as much as possible, or a product like Archival Mist, a de-acidification spray (a neutralizer). Simply coating each side with acrylic medium helps preserve paper, too.

Brushes

The diversity in brushes is staggering, from types of bristles to styles, shapes, and handle lengths.

These camel-hair brushes work well with gouache, tempera, inks, and watercolors.

You should experiment with a variety of brushes in different sizes. Try inexpensive foam and bristle brushes, daubers, even old toothbrushes and house painting brushes.

Shown here, from left to right, are a flat nylon brush, a #2 pointed nylon brush, an inexpensive house-painting brush, two sizes of foam brushes, a stencil dauber, a foam pouncer, a #1 watercolor mop brush, and a #1 flat watercolor wash brush.

Tools

Of course you'll need scissors, a brayer, and a craft knife. In addition, gel pens and a squirt bottle are convenient.

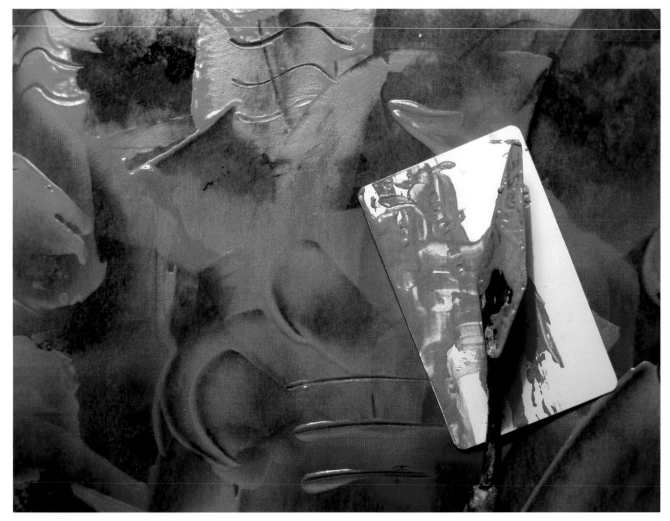

Old credit cards can be just as handy as painting knives.

Other tools that might come in handy include:

Assorted gadgets	Drinking straws	Ruler
Atomizer	Erasers	Scratch tools
Bamboo skewers	Eyedropper	Sponges
Blending stumps	Felt pads	Stencils
Blow dryer	Glue gun	Stencil brush
Bone folder	Heat gun	Squeegee
Charcoal	Hole punch	Squeeze bottles
China markers	Matboard scraps	Templates
Clothes iron	Palette knife	Tile adhesive spreader
Color shapers	Paper cutter	Wax crayons
Combs	Pencils	White-out pens
Cotton balls and swabs	Pencil sharpener	
Craft sticks	Putty knife	

Other Materials

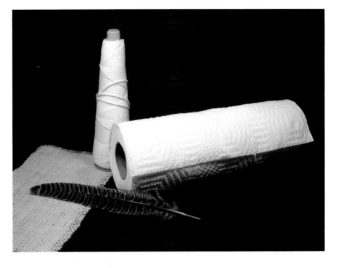

Besides optional project materials such as a papier-mâché box, a lampshade, or an art canvas, there are scores of other nifty items to use in art making. Many of them can be found in the household!

Useful art-making items:

Adhesives	Mylar
Bubble wrap	Painter's tape
Burlap	Palette
Cardboard	Paper towels
Cheesecloth	Paste waxes
Citra Solv	Patina solutions
Cutting mat	Plastic wrap
Doilies	Rags
Dryer sheets	Rubber cement
Drywall compound	Rubber gloves
Dura-Lar	Rubbing alcohol
Feathers	Salt
Foam core board	Sand
Gauze	Sandpaper
Gum arabic	Solvents
Gummed circles	Stickers
Lace	String
Lutrador	Textured rubber utensils
Masking fluid	Turpentine
Masking tape	Varnish
Metal foils	Water containers
Microbeads	Yupo

Even nail polish can become an art material! It's an acetone-based paint.

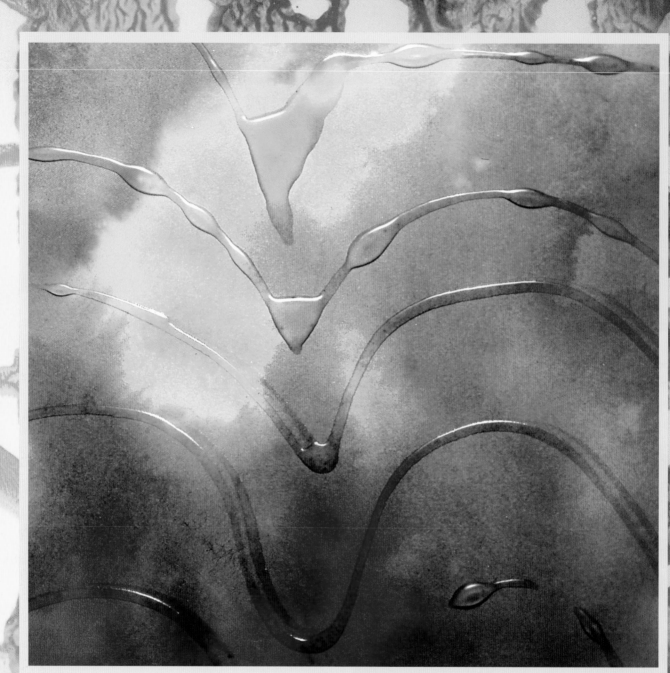

CHAPTER 2
Different Strokes

Think outside the box with glue, string, ketchup
bottles, and more for some unique designs.

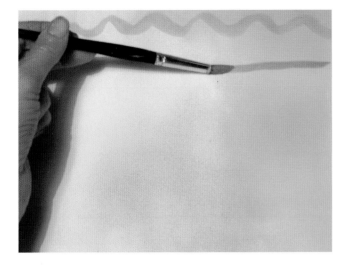

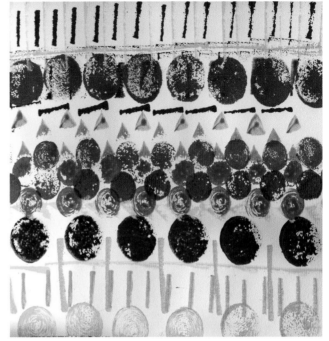

This design was done in tempera paint.

Lines and Shapes

Line is the most important design element, often enclosing or surrounding shapes. A line is any mark made on a surface with a moving point. A shape (an enclosed space) can be geometric, such as a triangle, rectangle, or circle. Free-form shapes are irregular and organic. You can create amazing decorated papers using just simple shapes and lines!

Getting into Shape

It's easy to paint shapes with foam brushes and daubers. Use the triangular tips at the sides of foam brushes. Or press foam alphabet letters into paint and stamp! Embellish a solid-color page or work on previously painted, multihued paper. (More about stamping in chapter 4.)

Foam letters were dipped in acrylic paint of various colors, including metallic gold.

> ### TIP TALK
> Thin papers will buckle and bulge after being painted. Even thick, heavy papers may warp. When wrinkled papers are dry, iron them on a low setting. Sandwich them between blotter papers if necessary. Or cover them with waxed paper and place a large, heavy book (or two) on top overnight.

Drawn Together

Try making marks or sketching with pastels, ink pens, or water-soluble pencils or crayons on painted paper. This wallpaper was enhanced with water-soluble pencils.

A fiber-tipped pen was used to draw these plants while the paper was wet.

Practice paint strokes with various sizes and types of brushes on both wet and dry paper. These lines were painted with gouache on drawing paper.

Play around with the dry-brush technique, too. This skimming method involves grazing the tips of bristles onto a surface.

Daub a fan brush into thick paint, or load any brush with "dryish" paint and spread the bristles with finger and thumb. Then hold the brush nearly parallel to the painting surface and drag lightly over the paper, just skimming the surface. A strié effect is produced.

Use dry-brushing with tempera, gouache, watercolor, acrylic, or oils.

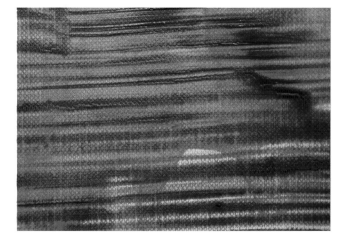

A Spattering of Inspiration

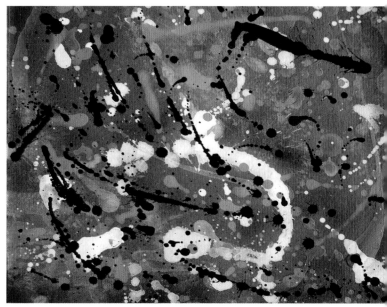

Drip and dribble some action paintings like famous artist Jackson Pollock's.

Paint spatters add visual texture. Try them on both dry and damp papers, especially where more interest is needed. Any water-based paint lends itself to spattering. Do two things first, though: Practice on scratch paper, and cover any areas that must remain untouched on the "good" paper.

Splatter up! An old toothbrush or any stiff brush is perfect for the job. Aim at the paper and push the bristles back with your thumb.

Paint specks in several colors make this book page far more appealing.

Squeeze Play

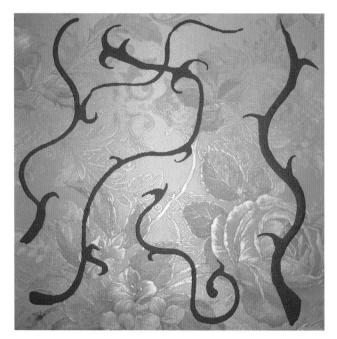

Paint writers and scribbler bottles make it easy to "draw" with paint. Puff paint, glossy squeeze paint, sparkly sequins writers, metallic writers—the variety of products available is astounding.

Make squiggles all over a page, or create intricate borders. Write out words and numbers, draw symbols, or sketch faces and figures. Do a few test lines on scrap paper first.

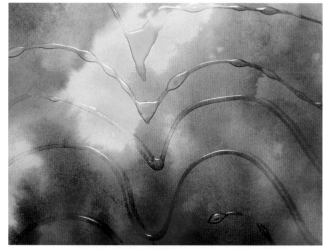

You can squeeze out lines and shapes with a bottle of white glue, too. Glue dries slightly raised on the surface, lending itself to several exciting treatments.

Wash over dried permanent glue with inks, watercolors, tempera, gouache, or thin acrylics. Enclosed "walls" of glue can hold a color separate from the rest, for a stained glass effect.

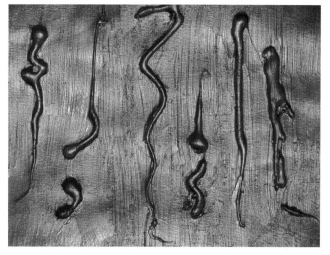

Instead of white glue, try clear school glue gel (the one that looks bluish in the bottle). This idea is especially striking on black paper.

When the extruded design dries, the transparent glue makes the black really "pop!" Now use chalk pastels in and around the design. Wow, right?

The black lines accent vivid, intense pastels very well.

Allow hot glue to cool before painting it. Copper paint was used here.

A dark wash "antiques" the copper.

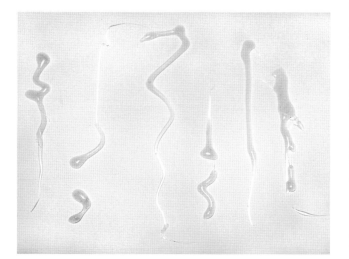

Experiment with colored or glitter glues, too—and how about a glue gun? Random squiggles of hot glue (on heavy paper) look a bit like solder after they've been covered with metallic paint!

A Glaze of Nice

Thin, transparent paint lends a veil of mystery to a surface. Many paint suppliers carry ready-mixed glazes, including metallic and iridescent glazes, and you can make your own quite easily, too.

GOING GREEN

Wash out empty ketchup or mustard squeeze bottles and use them for glue or paint.

Clean, recycled jars with shaker tops are nifty for sprinkling powdered tempera, salt, and more.

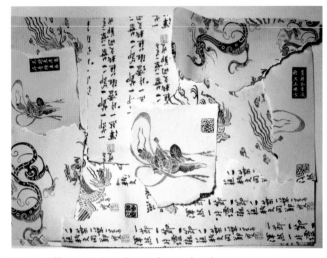

Three different Asian-themed scrapbook papers were torn and arranged atop a fourth page.

After the pieces were glued down, sheer layers of colors were washed over the collage to modify it.

With acrylics, create a glaze using paint mixed with water alone, or add liquid acrylic medium to paint. You will achieve better results with hues that are not opaque: Pthalo blue and pthalo green, azo yellow, dioxazine purple, alizarin crimson, and ultramarine blue are just some of the more transparent colors.

Apply glazes atop other (dry) painted areas, too. Oils (mixed with Liquin or other solvent) can be used to overlay a dry page.

These cut-out ladies were arranged and glued onto paper first.

A sheer golden ochre glaze was applied.

A brayer, often used in printmaking, is a hand roller that spreads ink thinly and evenly. You can buy rollers at the home improvement store to use as brayers. The large white paint roller cover is specifically for rag rolling. The brownish textured roller cover was used to decorate the paper shown.

When it was dry, ultramarine blue was added in some places, and then another golden layer after that.

On a Roll

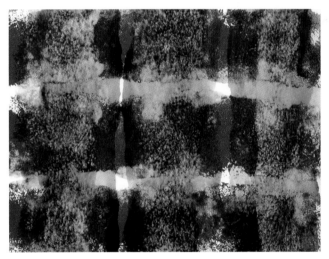

This inexpensive white paper was decorated with paint rollers.

Here are some nearly effortless background techniques. All you need (besides papers) is a brayer, a sheet of glass (tape the edges for safety's sake), and paint or ink. Oh, and maybe some scissors, string, and self-adhesive craft foam!

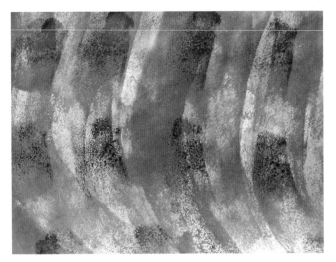

Even a smooth brayer can roll out attractive paintings. Color was rolled onto white paper here. Once the first layer was dry, two other colors were applied the same way.

Brayer-type printing can also be done with such homemade substitutes as a piece cut from a large foam swimming noodle! A section of 1-inch dowel (with finishing nails for handles) was run through the hole in its center. A woodburning tool, shown here, melted patterns into the foam. Caution: Work in a well-ventilated area when doing this.

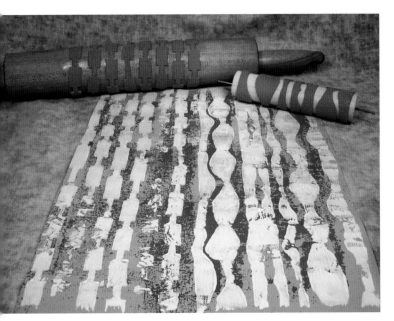

Self-adhesive foam craft strips, found in the kids' craft section, were applied to this kitchen rolling pin. I made a smaller textured roller by cutting a peel-and-stick foam sheet into shapes and applying the shapes to a 1-inch wooden dowel. If the pieces loosen from the rollers with use, adhere their edges with gel medium.

Another way to texturize a wooden roller is to wrap wire around it.

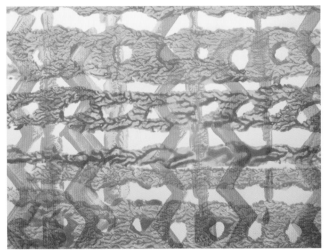

The roller shown above made this design in orange on paper that had been pre-stamped with sage-colored paint.

Even textured gel comfort grips on pencils can be used as mini-rollers. The one shown here was inked up with stamp pads.

This string/roller print on white paper was enhanced with water-soluble oil pastels.

String It Up (or Gouge It Out)

The 1-inch soft wooden dowel shown here was gouged with a tool used for carving linoleum and wood blocks. The "handles" at the ends are finishing nails.

If you wrap a hard rubber print roller with string, secure the string so it won't come unraveled. If your brayer comes apart for cleaning, wrapping rubber bands around the roller is easy!

Gouge out pieces of a cheap foam roller for a different effect.

Roll out paint or ink.

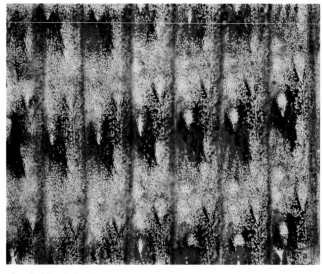

The finished design.

Project: Dimensional Flowers

Create everlasting flowers from paper you've decorated yourself. No watering required! There are numerous methods of making dimensional blossoms—I'll show you a simple one.

TOOLS & MATERIALS

- Pipe cleaners
- Beads with large holes
- Decorative paper
- Scissors
- Pencil
- Sharp, pointed tool
- Paint (optional)

On a plain sheet of paper, draw the outline of a five-petal flower about 6 inches
in diameter. Draw a 3- to 4-inch circle on
another sheet of paper. These will become
your patterns.

Use the patterns to cut out the flower and circle from two
different sheets of decorative paper. Poke a hole in the middle of each.

Fold a crease lengthwise in each petal of the flower and set
it aside. Cut 1-inch-long slits all around the circle, pointing
toward the center. Space the cuts about 1/4 inch apart.

Use a pencil and roll the fringe in toward the center of the circle. Touch up the curled fringe with paint if desired.

Tone down too-bright pipe cleaners, if you wish, by brushing on a bit of acrylic paint. Metallic gold was used here on the intense yellow and green pipe cleaners.

Place the rolled-up circle on top of the flower. Push a pipe cleaner through the center of both the flower and circle. String a bead onto the pipe cleaner on both sides of the flower. Crimp the pipe cleaner to hold the beads in place. Roll the leftover length of pipe cleaner into a coil.

Attach another pipe cleaner at the back of the flower for the stem.

Experiment with other petal shapes and sizes. This example sports two flower shapes together.

CHAPTER 3

Engaging Ways with Wet in Wet

Wet watercolors and inks diffuse in amazing ways on wet
surfaces. You can achieve soft, fluid effects with acrylics.

Bleeding and Blooms

The term for the spreading of color through wet paint or water is "bleeding." Pre-wet the paper for optimal results. Tip the painted paper in different directions to promote more blending and shifting of color.

Shown here are intense watercolors bleeding into each other on wet watercolor paper.

Inexpensive, non-colorfast crepe paper (and bright tissue paper) will bleed onto damp paper—use smooth white watercolor paper as the base. Cut or tear the colored

paper as desired. Lay a sheet of heavy glass over the top and allow the paper to dry overnight if you want to make a crepe paper print.

In this case, crumpled tissue paper was thoroughly dampened and imprinted onto paper.

It's Blooming Cool!

When wetness is added to a somewhat drier area, a "bloom" will likely occur. Blooms, aptly named for the flower heads they can resemble, can be quite lovely! Try creating them with clean water in a brush, dropped here and there into partially dry dark or intense color. Use watercolors, watery acrylics, dyes, or pigment inks.

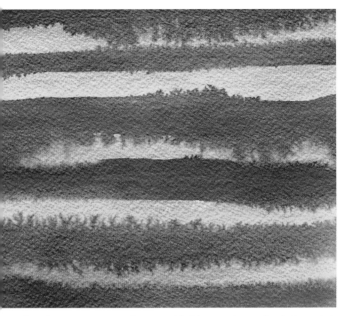

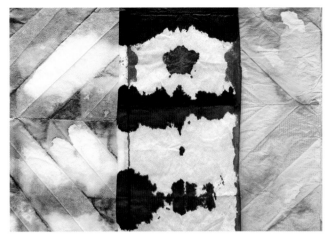

Another way to experiment with blossoming color is to paint stripes or shapes of very wet color directly alongside painted areas that haven't quite dried.

Exciting patterns can be obtained by folding, dipping, and painting. Gift wrap tissue can be used for fold-dyeing, but handle it extremely gingerly since it can be very fragile. Paper towels are sturdy, so do try them. Coffee filters or sturdy Japanese papers work best.

Tie-Dye Look-Alikes

Place liquid colorants (water-based ink, liquid watercolors, or dye) in shallow containers. Wear rubber gloves!

Fold or pleat the paper repeatedly until a small, compact rectangle or triangle is achieved. Then dip corners or edges into the liquid. Symmetrical designs will result. For a softer, blended effect, dampen the paper with water before dipping it into the colors.

If random dyeing is preferable to geometric folding, crumple or twist the paper arbitrarily instead.

After the paper is saturated with color, lay it on waxed paper or freezer paper to dry without opening the folds.

If desired later, refold the dry design and re-dip the edges in different colors. Or drop paint onto the folded, damp paper with a brush or an eyedropper.

This is a print from a dye-saturated paper towel. I simply pressed it onto a piece of construction paper.

Papers dyed with water-soluble colorants (watercolors, for example) will run if they are exposed to moisture later. If you need a tie-dyed paper that's bleed-proof, use thinned liquid acrylics, but open up acrylic-dyed paper (very carefully) *before* it dries to prevent sticking. Press dry papers with a warm iron to diminish creases.

I sprayed a white paper towel with water and brushed on fabric dyes. Even the freezer paper beneath it took on a colorful pattern!

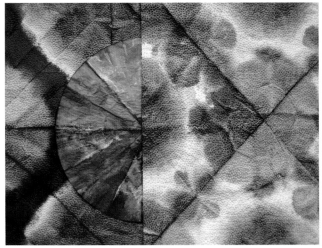

Metallic fluid acrylic was diluted with water for a bit of gold glitz. Two of the papers here are paper towels.

SMART ←→ SWAP

Using cotton balls to apply alcohol inks to paper (as a substitute for a store-bought applicator) isn't cost-effective, since they absorb a lot of ink. Try a scrap of felt instead.

Effects of Alcohol (Inks)

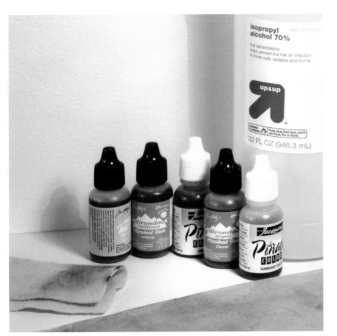

Directly applying these inks to absorbent paper results in blotches. Use slick, glossy paper or vellum instead to avoid blotching.

Dilute alcohol inks with blending solution or rubbing alcohol, if desired. A felt applicator can be very useful for obtaining soft results. If you want very subtle colors, use less ink and more blending solution or rubbing alcohol.

Are You Ready to Crumple?

Balled-up paper can be a sign of frustration in writing, yes, but here we scrunch it up with glee!

The simplest way to distress glossy paper is to crush it in your fist, open it carefully and flatten it somewhat, and run fine sandpaper over the surface. It's that easy!

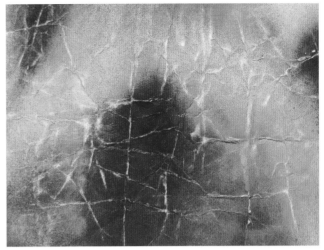

This heavy paper was spray-painted first. Then it was folded and sanded for added interest.

Batik-like "Cracks"

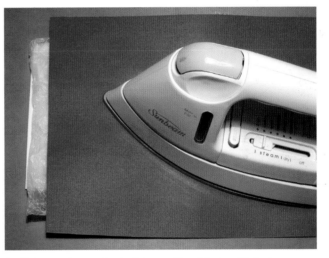

Batik is a resist method of decorating fabric with hot wax and dye baths. Painting over waxy areas on paper is also a resist method. (Stay tuned for more resist methods in chapter 8.)

Wad up waxed paper tightly, open it somewhat flat, and place it over cardstock or paper of choice. Arrange a cover sheet of scrap paper over that and press the three-layer "sandwich" with a hot clothes iron.

Remove the cover sheet and waxed paper. The cardstock or paper beneath will have received some of the wax. With a wide brush, gently wash on thin color.

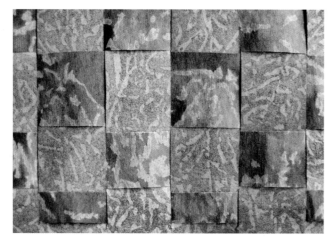

A paper weaving of strips made from two "batiks."

You can also cut shapes from the crumpled waxed paper. The waxed paper butterfly shape, at right, was ironed onto yellow-painted, dry paper. When the wax cooled, other colors were washed on.

Crush and Crease

Here's another simple way of creating a batik effect: Crumple any fairly firm paper into a ball, open it up carefully, and run an inked stamp pad lightly over the surface. Even ordinary waxed paper is easily decorated this way!

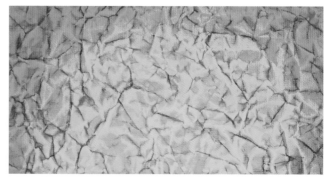

For paper that creases when crumbled, use a wide, flat brush instead of a stamp pad. Merely dampen the brush with paint, dye, or ink; don't saturate it. Skim the raised surfaces with a dry-brush technique. Don't force the paint into the crevices of the paper.

This pastels paper worked well for this technique.

Let the paper dry. Rescrunch it and repeat with another color, highlighting the raised portions from a different direction. In this example, brown kraft paper was brushed with metallic gold tempera paint and coppery acrylic paint.

While the paint is still wet, press a sheet of paper onto it. Brayer the back or use the flat of a hand to ensure good contact. Peel the page from the glass. Instant texture! Try it with more paper and other colors, lifting in different directions to produce variety.

Multiple colors make a showy design.

Yet another way to show off the "hills and valleys" of scrunched-up paper is with spray paint! Work outdoors (or in a well-ventilated area) and wear a protective mask when using spray paints. Lay down protective coverings against overspray.

Flatten crinkled paper somewhat. Select an aerosol color that contrasts well with the paper color. Hold the spray can very low and horizontally, shooting across the paper from one direction only.

Even after being ironed flat, this page will look remarkably like it does here.

When the page is dry, run a Paintstik or oil pastel (in a contrasting color) over the "bumps" for even more dazzle. The ridges here were accentuated with white and dark oil pastel.

Lift and Separate

This technique, sometimes called "pulling," is a textural variation of the monoprint method we will discuss on page 60.

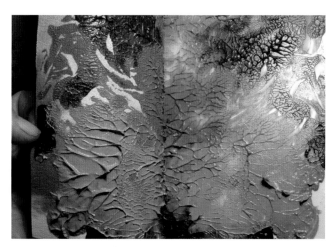

TIP TALK

It's also possible to make two textured copies at once—mirror images of each other. Simply paint or ink up one of the pages first (instead of a glass printing plate) and press the second sheet on top. Pull apart carefully. Veined or feathery patterns will appear.

Mix acrylic paint with heavy gel medium. Coat a sheet of glass with the mixture using a brush or paint roller. The heavier the application, the more pronounced the resulting texture will be.

Project: Pushing the Envelope

Have you ever forgotten to buy a greeting or birthday card for someone? Now you can whip one up in no time! I'll guide you in fashioning a basic type of stationery.

TOOLS & MATERIALS

- Decorative papers
- Pencil and eraser
- Metal ruler
- Scissors
- Bone folder (a tool used for scoring and creasing paper)
- Adhesive (glue stick or white craft glue)
- Store-bought sticker (optional)
- Craft knife and cutting mat (optional)

What a Card!

This project is an all-in-one card and envelope.

I suggest creating a card that will be approximately 4 by 5½ inches when finished. Begin by tracing the pattern on the opposite page lightly in pencil on either side of a decorative sheet that's about 10 by 13 inches.

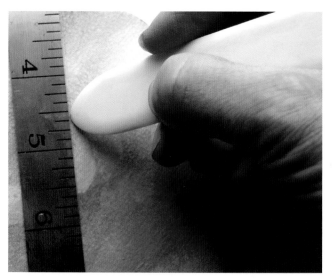

Cut out the pattern shape. Erase any pencil marks that show. Working on the decorative outside of the envelope, score where the dotted lines appear on the template by running the tip of the scissors or a pointed bone folder along the metal ruler edge. Scoring breaks the top fibers of the paper enough to produce crisp folds.

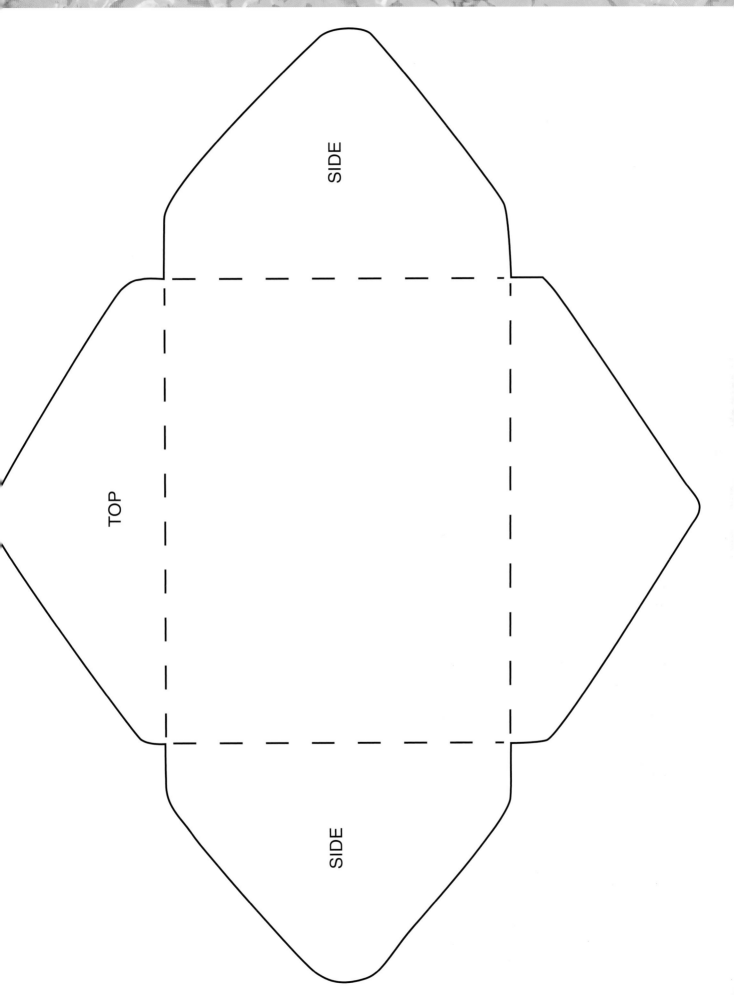

Next, fold the paper and press the creases flat with the bone folder to sharpen the folds.

Cut a 3 by 4½ inch square of white or light-colored paper to use as the card insert. This will be centered and glued inside to hold a personal message. A slightly larger coral sheet was glued behind the insert shown here to serve as a border. Enhance the inside of the envelope as you wish, but keep the total thickness to no more than ¼ inch to meet postal regulations.

If the front of the card is dark, either lighten the return and address areas with paint (as shown here) or stick on your own address labels. You can also use a white pen to address a dark card. Sakura Gelly Roll pens in white work well on most dark papers.

When you're ready to mail the card, use a ready-made sticker to seal the flaps together on the back, or glue on a small piece of decorated paper to close the back.

These blank mini-books by artist Kelly Face are shown with some of the materials needed to make them. Research simple bookbinding and use your decorated papers on the covers!

CHAPTER 4

Masking, Stamping, and Scraping

In this chapter, we'll spray, stencil, scrape, sponge,
and even stomp! I'll also show you how
to make your own unique printing stamps.

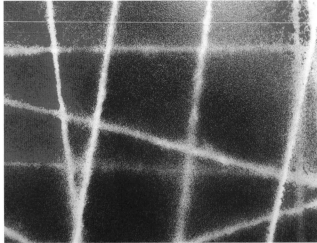

These lines were created by wrapping cardstock with yarn and spray-painting over it. Put the wrapped card on newspapers outdoors and spray away! Wait until the paint is dry before removing the yarn or string.

Have a Ball with Masks

Choose from many ways to make shapes on paper using masks and stamping tools. "Mask," as an art term, refers to a material that is placed over paper or paint to preserve it, preventing its exposure to more paint media. Highlights are often retained this way. Repositionable paper numbers and symbols can be used as masks.

Cut shapes from tagboard, or use die-cut shapes, real leaves—anything thin, flat, and in silhouette. Hold the shape firmly in place on paper of choice. Brush paint from the center of the shape right past the edges, pushing the paint onto the paper. (Note that the "hole," the tagboard from which the note was cut, was also used here as a stencil. One can spray-paint through stencils, too.)

TIP TALK

For stenciling and masking, use stencil paint, oils, or thick, heavy-bodied acrylics.

Leaves (positive shapes) formed the masks that were edged here with acrylic paint.

A feather was used repeatedly, with a soft foam roller and acrylic paint, on white paper.

Stick-ons and Reverse Stencils

Try masking off portions of sturdy glossy or coated paper with self-adhesive products. Burnish the edges for a good seal. Stroke thin paint or ink over all and allow the paper to dry completly before removing the masks.

Self-adhesive shapes may be difficult to remove, even on sturdy, slick paper. Rather than tearing the paper, leave them there if you must (especially if they have absorbed color differently than did the support).

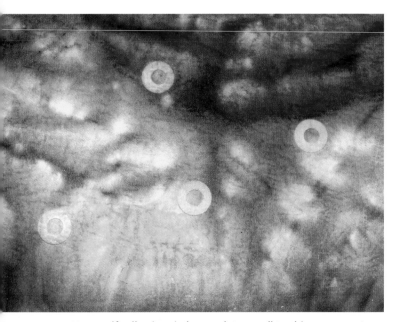

Or rub crayons or oil pastels outward from masks. Try chalk pastels too.

Here, self-adhesive circles stuck too well to this paper, so I simply left them on.

Using oil pastels heavily near the edges of tagboard shapes allows you to smear and blend the color from the mask to the paper. Use thumb pressure!

I held a soft chalk pastel broadside and ran it off the edges of a torn paper shape.

Soften the gradation with your fingers or with blending stumps.

Spray over leaves, let them dry, reposition them, and then spray with another color.

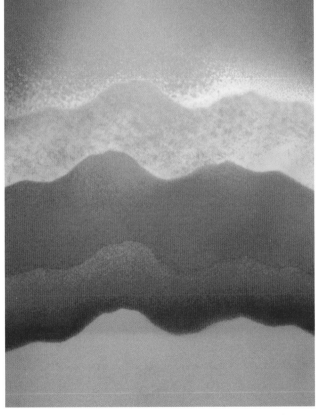

You can also spray aerosol colors off the edge of a mask. In this example, a simple tagboard edge was used repeatedly.

While these holographic borders are nice in and of themselves, they can be arranged on a page to serve as masks . . .

. . . and removed after the spray paint has dried. Repeat as desired with other spray-on colors.

Stuck-on borders on white paper have been spray-painted over with copper.

The white shapes that remained were later colored with alcohol inks.

Conventional Stenciling

Stencils and open-work templates might be called masks, too. Paint or printing ink is applied through their cut-out areas onto the paper. Commercial stencils are easy to use, especially with daubers, pouncers, or stencil brushes. Die-cut scrapbooking sheets or sequin waste make good stencils, too. Sequin waste, also called punchinella, is the holey plastic ribbon that's left over when a manufacturer punches out sequins. You can buy the ribbon at a craft supply store.

You can also design original stencils. Trace your own pattern or shape onto heavy paper or a stencil sheet and cut it out. Use a craft knife with care, atop a cutting mat.

Hold stencils in place with painter's tape, liquid stencil adhesive, or repositionable adhesive spray. Use "dry" paint, not juicy, and apply it with a daubing motion.

Try various color combinations and paint types, from heavy-bodied acrylics or oils to spray paints or stencil creams.

Make a raised design by spreading molding paste or thick paint over stencil openings. Joint compound works, too.

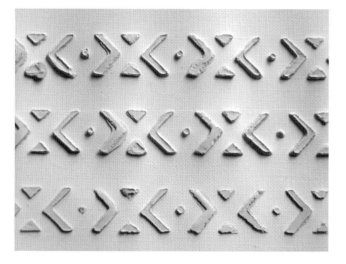

When the design is dry, apply and then wipe off thin, dark paint to accentuate the texture.

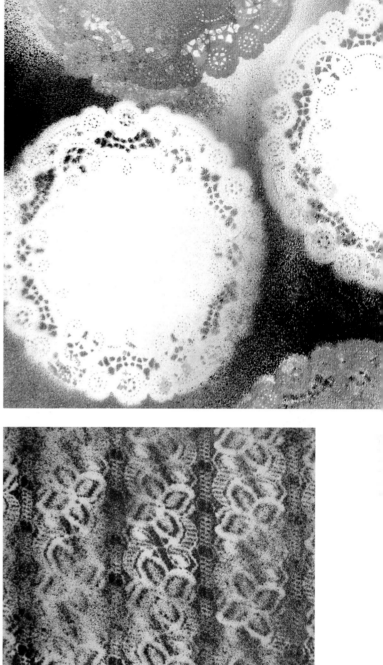

Even paper doilies or lace can become stencils of sorts. I created these designs on white paper with spray-paint.

Inspector Gadget Printing

There are many types of found objects you can print or stamp with. Even hand- and footprints can be decorative! On the paper in this photo, I stamped with silicone kitchen trivets and through a sequin waste ribbon.

Instant Pattern

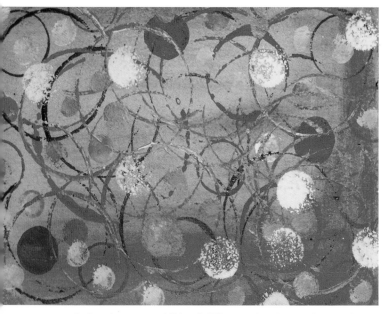

Dip bottle caps and lids of different sizes into paints and press onto paper repeatedly.

Stamping is child's play, yes, but the results can be excellent. This pattern was made with the raised design on a vintage rubber bathing cap.

Roll or brush paint (or printing ink) onto textured found objects and press them to paper. Thick lace, burlap, corrugated rubber or cardboard, kitchen utensils—the choices are infinite. Try tempera, gouache, and acrylic paint. Here, a piece of rubber tread was rolled up with acrylic paint on one side and printed.

Then the other side of the rubber piece was inked and printed.

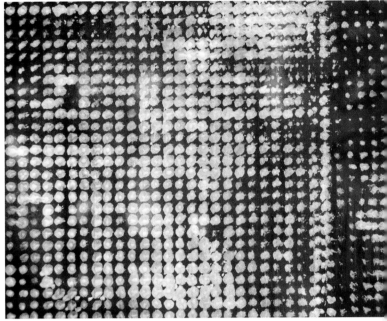

A non-slip rubber shelf liner was painted with acrylics and pressed onto drawing paper. Bath mats and textured place mats work, too!

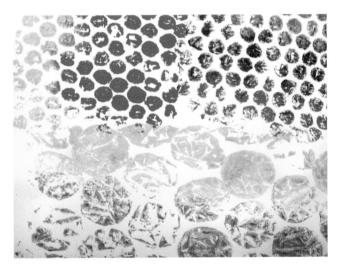

The raised surface of bubble wrap was painted, and paper was pressed onto it while the paint was still wet.

You can make your own "rubber stamps" using foam core board as a base. Stick on self-adhesive foam letters or shapes and seal the surface with gel medium. Remember that the stamped image will be a mirror image, reversed from the original.

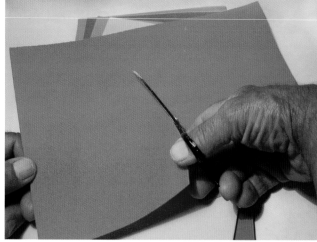

Crafters' foam sheets are easily cut for block printing. Similar products include Foamtastic, a store-bought art product, and Mastercarve, an artists' carving block.

This homemade stamp, made with craft foam, was used repeatedly on a gold-threaded Unryu paper.

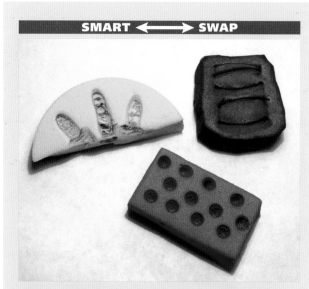

These small printing stamps were cut from larger foam shapes—children's toys. They were altered with a wood-burning tool and/or a wood-carving tool. And don't forget that you can carve rubber erasers, and even potatoes!

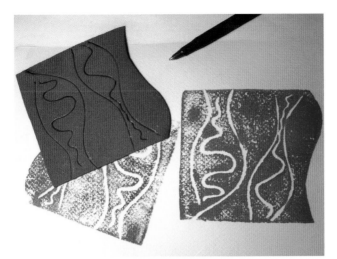

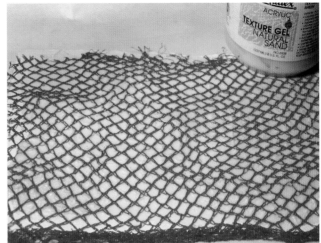

Another easy way to use foam sheets is to press designs into them with the tip of a ballpoint pen. Simply draw a pattern deeply into the sheet, roll printing ink or paint onto it, and press it onto paper. Re-ink and print multiple times on the same page, if you wish, with multiple colors!

When the print is dry, you can enhance it with oil pastels, colored pencils, markers, watercolors, or soft chalk pastels.

After thoroughly pressing mesh fabric into a layer of texture gel or stucco medium, let it dry at least fifteen minutes before removing the mesh.

Here, I added acrylic washes in several colors to finish the project.

A different approach is to put down a layer of gesso, stucco medium, or heavy gel medium on sturdy paper. While the layer is still wet, stamp it with textured objects. When the gesso or gel is dry, paint it. Later, apply thin, darker paint. It will pool in the indentations and add impact. Here, a wash of liquid acrylic reveals the impressions that were made in white gesso.

A nylon mesh vegetable bag was pressed into stucco medium on cardstock and removed after it hardened. Then thin acrylic washes were applied.

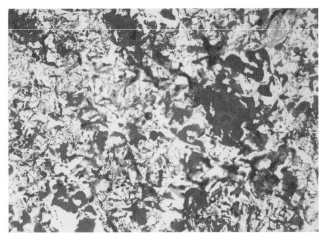

A bath pouf is a good stand-in for a sponge. Even a wad of crumpled-up waxed paper (used here) makes an interesting applicator!

Sponges, Shoes, and Such

A natural sea sponge was the tool of choice here, but you can tear a synthetic one into smaller, irregular pieces for a similar effect. Simply pat the sponge lightly into one or more colors of paint, dye, or ink and press it onto paper. Repeat until the desired effect is achieved. For extra pizzazz, sponge lightly with a final layer of metallic acrylic paints (that's what added the sparkle to this example).

Sponging paint through mesh or gauze creates even more interest.

Try cutting flat synthetic sponges into nifty shapes, dipping them into paint, and stamping repeatedly onto paper. These shapes were cut from a cellulose sponge. The paper was a ready-made patterned sheet.

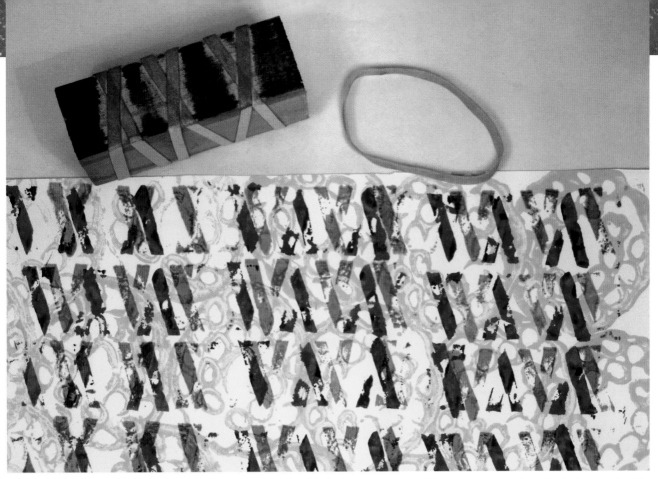

Or wrap rubber bands around a block of wood for another kind of texture stamp. This example, preprinted in beige paint with a found object, was finished with a rubber-banded block and stamp pads.

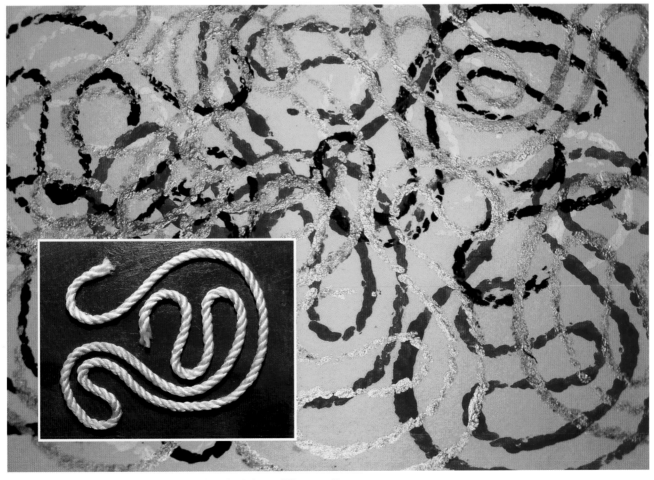

Try gluing string or cord flat on a wooden block for a different effect.

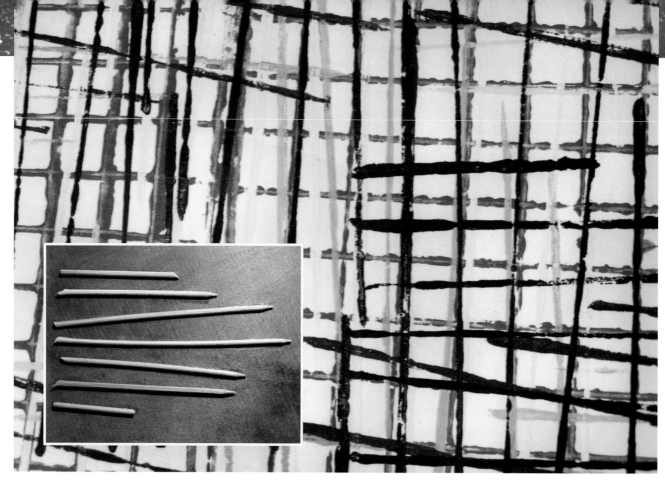

Bamboo skewers were cut and glued onto a wood block to make a useful stamp.

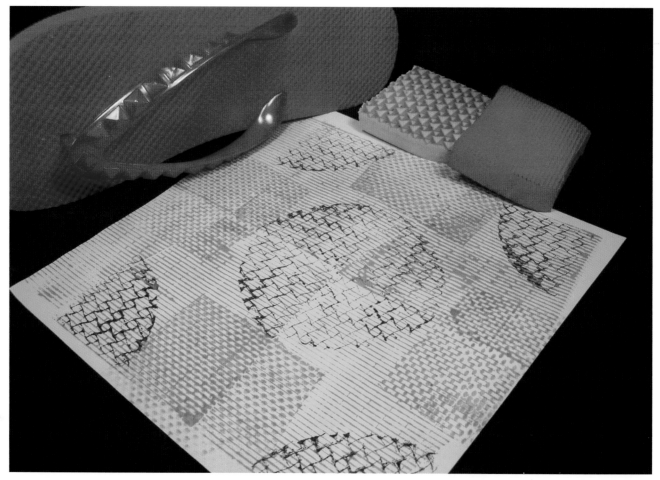

Low-cost flip-flops can be cut up with a sharp utility knife and used as stamping tools. Their textured bottoms are ready to use as is. The decorated page here was done with three flip-flop stamps with different tread patterns inked with stamp pads.

The smooth top side of flip-flop foam can be molded with a heat gun. First, arrange some flat items on a hard surface: buttons, paper clips, safety pins, washers, and the like. Apply heat to the foam piece (don't hold the piece in your hand!) for about twenty seconds. Quickly, before it cools, press it onto the items. Apply intense, even pressure for about twenty seconds.

The stamp in the middle was made with novelty buttons. Their backs were removed so they would lie flat.

Another way to print patterns is to ink up a piece of wallpaper that has a raised design. Use either a brayer or a large, flat foam brush to spread the paint or ink on the wallpaper. Press rice paper or tissue paper onto it and lift. Repeat with another color if you wish, changing the orientation.

Leaf It to Printing

Paint fresh leaves on the veined side to decorate paper with a nature motif.

The soles of athletic shoes usually have wonderful patterns, so roll an inked brayer over one and step on it!

Hand and bare foot prints are nifty, too—use non-toxic paint for this fancy footwork. You can also use a pet's paw prints, but wash and dry those feet *thoroughly* afterward.

Use a brush or sponge to coat a leaf with color. (Or apply paint to leaves with a brayer.)

Quickly place the leaf, inked side down, on the paper to be printed. Cover with newsprint. Hold the cover paper firmly in place and either press with the flat of your hand or use a clean brayer to roll over the paper.

Lift the leaves from the paper before they dry completely, since they might stick.

Absorbing Imprinting

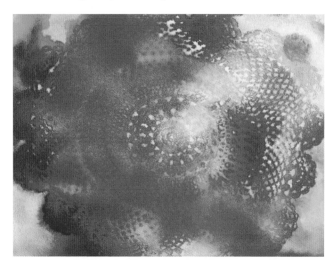

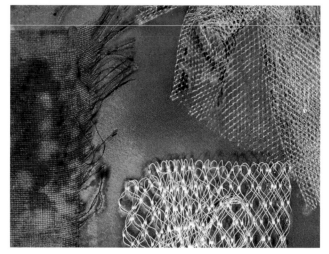

Lay them out flat on damp, smooth watercolor paper, and saturate them with wet, rich watercolor, ink, or dye. Lay a piece of heavy glass on top if necessary for good contact. After a day or two, lift them up, and you'll see a likeness!

Select thick string, bits of crocheted or lacy material, or other absorbent, textured materials.

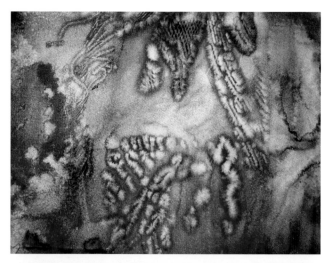

Shards of window glass were set into wet watercolor paint with a heavy book on top and left overnight. A fragmented design resulted. (Handle broken glass with caution.)

Grasses and fresh leaves make fabulous organic designs. Fabric dye was used here on watercolor paper.

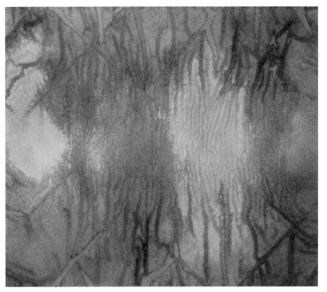

Here is how it looked after the waxed paper was removed the next day.

Apply a sheet of waxed paper over juicy watercolor or thinned acrylic. Then let dry with or without a large, heavy book on top. (Try it both ways.) By the next day the wrinkled pattern likely will be awesome. You can also try pleating the waxed paper first (pressing folds into it). Open it up again before using it to print. In this photo, wet fabric dyes on watercolor paper are ready for the creased waxed paper (upper left).

Plastic cling wrap works very well, too. Make sure the piece of food wrap is large enough to cover the paper even after it's pinched and folded. Again, spread it upon very wet, brilliant paint or ink. Nip in a few creases and crinkles. The effect will look similar to that of shards of glass. It's not necessary to place weight on top. Allow the piece to dry undisturbed overnight.

The finished plastic-wrap print, using liquid fabric dye on watercolor paper.

Here, thinned acrylic paints were allowed to dry under wrinkled plastic wrap.

Scraping By and Feeling Groovy

Surfaces can be grazed, scratched, and abraded in several ways, somewhat smoothly or quite the opposite. In this case, wax crayon was layered heavily on a piece of paper before a design was scraped into it.

Go Ahead, Be Pushy!

Move paint around with a scraping tool—you can use anything from a putty knife or spatula to an old credit card.

For a colored background, use colored cardstock or paint a base color first and allow it to dry.

Squirt acrylic paints here and there and "squeegee" them in different directions while still wet. Also experiment with tube watercolors, thick tempera, or tube gouache on paper that's neither too wet nor too dry. Give oils a go, too.

Next, use a flat scraper on the clear surface, spreading the colors beneath. You can produce some wild and crazy papers this way.

Watercolor on a presoaked sheet of watercolor paper was scraped with a rectangular piece of plexiglass.

A fun modification is to squeeze out lumps of paint on a page and then cover the whole thing with clear self-adhesive contact paper.

Another variation is to scratch into thick black gesso while it is still wet.

After the gesso dries, wash over it with thinned metallic or interference paint, and wipe the raised surface immediately.

Marvelous Monoprinting

A monoprint is a one-of-a-kind print (essentially a printed painting).

Apply an even, thin-to-medium coat of tube acrylic paint or printing ink to a glass pane. (If, when you print it, the color spreads too much, you'll know you used too much paint.)

Immediately scrape a design into the wet surface on the glass. Combs and grouting tools make exciting designs; a straight-edged scrap of matboard works too!

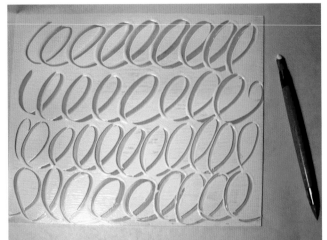

A variation on scraping is to draw directly on the wet printing plate with utensils or sticks. Rubber-tipped shaper tools work well for this step.

Place smooth paper face-down onto the plate and rub the flat of your hand all over the back. Press firmly, although too much pressure will move the paint. Peel the paper from the plate. Let paper dry.

You can create a more complex design, if you wish, by printing over it again.

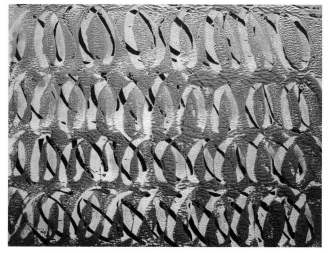

The loopy design made with white block-printing ink was allowed to dry, then the paper was off-set and reprinted with a similar design in silver ink.

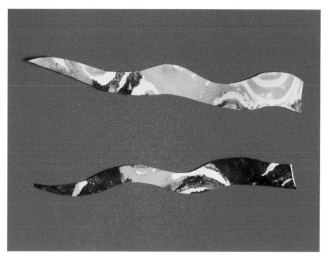

The paper masking shapes can be used in another project.

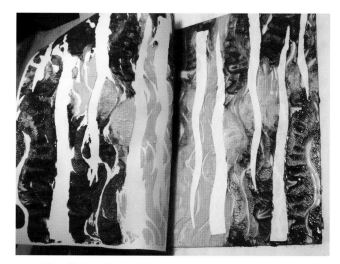

Consider placing flat masks atop an inked design on the printing plate. Paper shapes scattered here and there before printing will leave voids in the design. In this example, a layer of acrylics on glass was scratched, and then paper shapes were placed on top of the paint before the print was pulled. Note the white spaces in the print, mirroring the paper pieces.

After a print has dried, you can add other art media if the page needs something extra. Fill in the exposed paper portions of a print with oil pastel, as shown here, or with markers, colored pencils, or chalk pastels.

Finally, here's another monoprinting idea using black gesso and aluminum foil. Heavy-duty foil is sturdier, of course, but not an absolute requirement. You'll also need black gesso, a brayer, a pencil, and white or light-colored paper.

Roll a thin coat of black gesso all over the tin foil. Let the gesso just barely begin to dry—just until the shine is fading.

Peel the foil off. The graphic impact of the black-and-white design can be compelling just as it is.

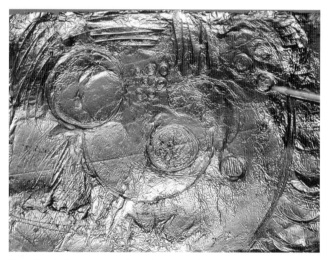

Turn the foil over and place it gesso-side-down on the paper. Draw a design in the foil with a blunt pencil, covering the page with lines, patterns, and shapes.

Or you can embellish the page with color after the gesso is dry. Use paints, colored inks, colored pencils, or oil or chalk pastels—your choice.

Scraping Gel, Gesso, or Modeling Paste

Apply a thin coat of modeling or molding paste first, and scuff it around a bit. Gel medium or thick gesso can be substituted for modeling paste.

SMART ⟷ SWAP

Joint compound can be used instead of molding paste, too. You can find it at building supply stores.

Instead of scraping, try writing in a layer of heavy gel medium. When it's dry, apply a dark stain and wipe the surface clean. Make your own "antiquing" solution by diluting acrylic paint with water.

Roughing It

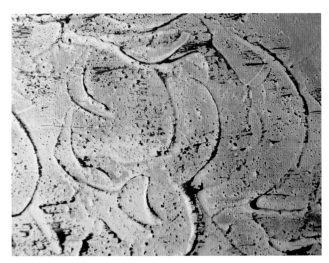

Thick Sludge is swirled on with a twisting motion of a painting knife to texturize heavy paper. Sludge is an acrylic extender from TriArt and is made from recycled materials.

In this instance, when the surface was dry, light color was washed on and, later, dark acrylic paint was grazed onto the surface to enhance the paper further.

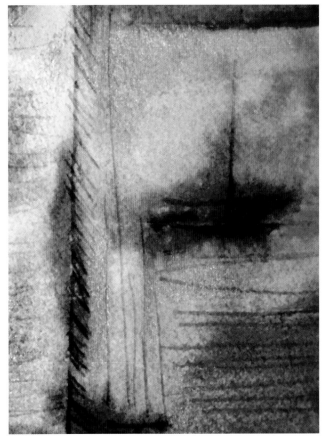

You can also scuff up paper using the debossing technique. Wash over smooth watercolor paper with watercolor paint, ink, or thin acrylics. While the paint is still damp, press lines into the paper with a sharp instrument. The scratches (indentations) should "take" the paint better, creating darker lines that contrast with the smooth paper.

The pointed tool used here was a bamboo stick.

Then layer darker colors on top. A scratch tool reveals the contrasting tones.

Here's another type of sgraffito (scratching into a surface). Dorland's Wax Medium, a translucent compound of waxes and resin, can be mixed with acrylic or oil paints or with powdered pigments. Applied thinly to a sturdy paper, it takes scratched marks very well, as shown in this example.

Pattern Play with Paste

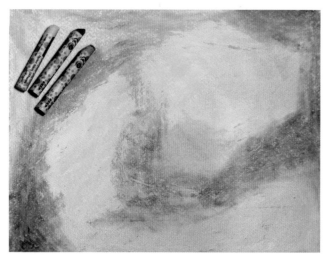

Or you can scratch through oil pastels. Apply lighter colors first, as shown here.

Paste papers, with their rich, dimensional designs, date back centuries. In the past, cooked pastes were the norm. They often involve cornstarch and boiling water, and they typically dry shinier than uncooked pastes. The procedure here does not call for a stove. Furthermore, the "paste" can even be made of thick acrylic paint alone, if you don't want to use a thickening agent such as art paste.

Heavy-bodied acrylics were manipulated to create this design.

Mix in water-based paint or ink until the desired color is reached. Spread a bit of paste onto scratch paper to test.

Select a piece of strong, non-absorbent paper for the substrate for this project. Spread the paste mixture smoothly onto the substrate page with a house-painting brush or a wide foam brush. (Feel free to mix up paste batches of several colors and apply them to a single sheet!)

To make a small amount of paste, put 1/2 teaspoon wheat paste, art paste, or wallpaper paste powder into a container. Add 1/2 cup water and whisk out the lumps. Add small amounts of more powder, stirring, until the mixture is no longer watery, but not too thick (it should be the consistency of cake batter). Letting it sit for about half an hour will help thicken it.

Draw forks, wide-tooth hair combs, or other utensils through the thick paint. Cut notches into stiff cardboard or plastic for homemade serrated tools. Tile adhesive spreaders make great lines, too.

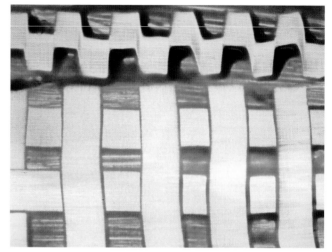

Try various wavy or straight patterns.

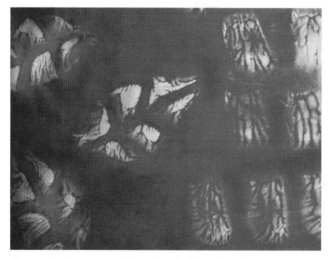

Instead of making the paste yourself, you can buy commercial products such as Elmer's Art Paste. Mix it with water according to the package directions to create a thick paste. Colourcraft's Brusho Thickener is a similar product. The latter was used on this page.

Here's another idea to try: After one layer is dry, paint a different color of paste over the first and comb in an additional design. Or use colored paper as the base and layer it with a contrasting color of paste.

Alternatively, try stamping a hard object into the wet mixture to displace the paste. That was done at the left side of this design. At the right, a large brush was slapped against the surface repeatedly.

If a scraped design is unsatisfactory, there is an easy fix: While the paper is still wet, smooth the paste out and comb in a new design.

Paste paper takes a fairly long time to dry. Hang it up or lay it flat. Store leftover paste covered in the refrigerator. Keep out of the reach of children.

Project: An Altered Book Journal

No binding, no sewing, and a discarded book finds a new life—what a deal!

TOOLS & MATERIALS

- Gel medium
- Brushes
- An unwanted, sturdy hardcover book
- Old credit card
- Craft knife
- Decorative papers and waxed paper
- Gesso
- Paints, markers, pencils, and other art media
- Fabric, photos, ephemera (written or printed matter originally meant to be short-lived, such as greeting cards, postcards, and ticket stubs), and more

Cut or tear out every third page of the book, to make room for decorative papers and keepsakes.

If the pages are thin, laminate some of them together for added strength. Use gel medium with a wide foam brush, and smooth the laminated pages with a credit card. Let dry. Separate sets of glued-together pages from the rest of the book with a sheet of waxed paper before proceeding.

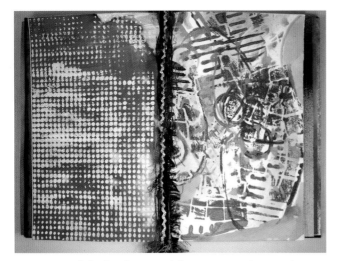

Two pages of the book opened flat—a "spread"—can be covered with a single, large, decorative paper. Crease the paper at the center and trim the edges so that the spread will open and close properly later on. Adhere using the same technique as before.

Of course two different decorative papers can be applied to facing pages, too. Cover the seam in the middle with fabric, yarn, or colored tape.

Glue on dark-colored tissue shapes if you wish to shade an area. There are many types of white ink pens on the market for making marks on dark backgrounds.

To make areas on the decorative pages for writing or sketching with dark colors, wash thinned gesso in some places. Or paint in some shapes with light-colored acrylics. Journaling in dark ink will show up better against the backdrop of these lighter spaces. When the gesso or paint is dry, write, stamp, or doodle away! There are no rules about what else to add to the pages. Ticket stubs, maps, lists, sketches, even memorable words are all fair game.

While the original book cover can be left as is, you may wish to paint, embellish, or re-cover it.

TIP TALK

Alter a book that's already about a topic that speaks to you, if possible. For example, choose an unwanted travel book if your journal will include your own travels. Preserving the title or incorporating some of the words, passages, or pictures into your artwork will be easy!

(Of course you can decorate the pages of a blank journal, instead. Glue your own decorative papers onto the bare pages, and/or paint them as you please.)

CHAPTER 5
Frottage and
Reverse Frottage

Frottage is the rubbing of a design or pattern onto
paper from a textured surface. You'll discover several
ways to use this easy technique in this chapter.

Rubbings Are Child's Play

Crayons make for quick and colorful artwork on lightweight paper over fresh leaves, coins, lace, doilies, or other flat, textured items. You can also use oil pastel sticks (here, on tissue) instead of wax crayons.

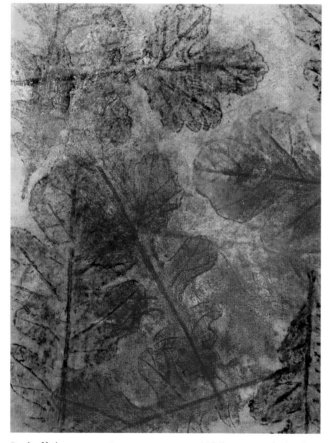

Peel off the crayons' paper wrappers. While textured plastic rubbing plates are available commercially, you can simply arrange textured articles on a table or other hard, smooth

surface. Lay paper on top (try copy or tracing paper) and hold in place while rubbing a crayon broadside. Vary colors as desired.

Watercolor was washed over the rubbing on the paper pictured here. The wax crayon resisted the paint. (Learn more resist techniques in chapter 8.)

Sanding Is a Cinch

Removing magazine color over a stencil-shape results in a negative image, a sort of inverse frottage.

Choose a dark, colorful magazine page sturdy enough to withstand the abrasion process. On a hard surface, arrange relatively flat, firm templates or stencils and place the paper on top. Hold the magazine page and the stencil in place with one hand while rubbing with fine sandpaper with the other.

Clean off the dust with a damp cloth.

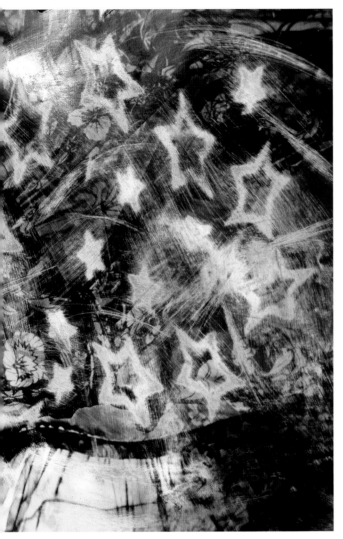

In this instance, after the sanding was done, acrylic paint was added back into areas that required definition. Notice the template and corrugated cardboard (top left in photo) used with this page.

Abrade unwanted text right off the page! You may go right through very thin papers, so consider adhering them to another page first. Allow the glue to dry before sanding the page.

TIP TALK

Sometimes the printed word in assorted sizes and fonts can add variety and interest. Text can make for powerful pages at times.

Acrylic paint was added here and there to enhance this design, too.

Try Tarnish Remover

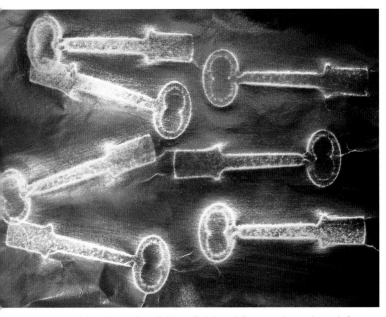

A bit of metal-polishing fluid and fine steel wool work for this technique, too. Here, foil paper functioned well.

Thin magazine papers present a challenge, because they tear easily. Coins were placed underneath this page to make it more unusual.

Project: Covering a Keepsake Box

Round, oval, rectangular, or square, a decorative vessel can be very useful for stowing mementos or other items. Cover a recipe box, jewelry box, mailbox, lunch box, or hatbox. This method is a snap!

TOOLS & MATERIALS:

- Lidded wooden or papier-mâché box
- Decorative papers
- Craft knife and/or scissors
- Ruler or paper-cutter
- Cutting mat (optional)
- Primer/gesso
- Ribbon, beads, and so on (optional)
- Adhesive
- Acrylic paint
- Brushes
- Acrylic medium

Turn your decorative paper facedown and trace the shape of the box lid. Do the same for the sides, rotating the box and tracing the top and bottom edges of the entire circumference as one shape. The long strip in this photo will be used to cover the sides of the box shown. The same treatment can be done with the lid edge, or you can cover it with ribbon instead.

It's better to cut the decorative paper shapes ever so slightly smaller than the box, rather than larger. Priming the box is optional, but painting its edges with acrylic paint in a matching color will disguise small gaps later. When all the edges are dry, coat the box (or the lid) with adhesive and apply the decorative papers.

Even a tin will do, especially if the metal is roughened first with sandpaper! They cost very little at thrift shops.

Allow the adhered papers to dry overnight, and then apply several protective coats of acrylic medium. If you want, add a knob or embellish the vessel with costume jewelry, beads, seashells, feathers, buttons, or other ornaments.

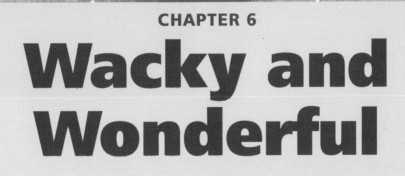

CHAPTER 6

Wacky and Wonderful

Now for some madcap, zany art making.
The techniques in this section are wild and quirky!

A Pinch of Powders

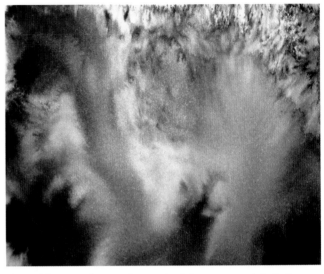

The cold-water dye used to make this page was labeled "olive green." The multihued granules were sprinkled onto wet, smooth watercolor paper.

Dyes in Dry Form

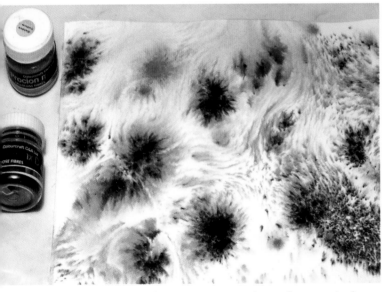

The particles in dry concentrates and crystals can make for exquisite effects on damp paper.

Crystals: Not Powders, Exactly

Instant tea or coffee, anyone? And I've already mentioned that walnut inks also come in crystal form. Colors in crystal form like these make interesting effects on paper.

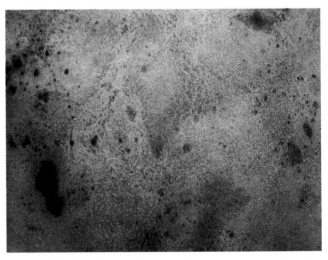

Powdered instant tea on damp watercolor paper produced this effect

Dropping and Smearing

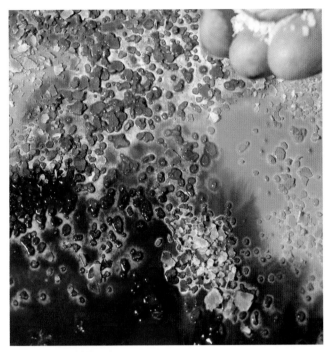

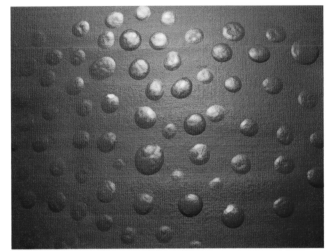

Oh, for a Margarita! Sprinkle crystals of table salt, kosher salt, or rock salt into wet watercolors. Experiment with acrylic washes, too.

Dribble, drip, or drop for some great effects! For the project in this photo, acrylic paint was mixed with acrylic gel medium using a palette knife to blend out all the lumps. Then it was put into a squeeze bottle (a small-nozzled one is best) and applied to a painted page in a raised, dotted pattern.

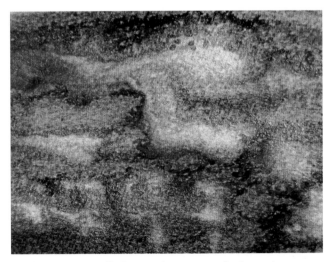

Salt leaves lighter spots behind because it dehydrates the paint. Allow it to dry, undisturbed. When the salt is brushed off, a starry pattern should be visible.

Try dropping metallic latex paint—copper is shown here—into wet acrylic inks.

Eyedroppers and Pipettes Perform

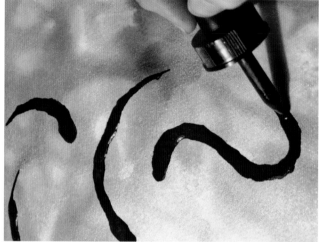

Here's how to make the marks: On a background of choice, draw lines with an eyedropper or pipette filled with ink.

These marks were made with acrylic inks and a fan brush.

Stroke over the ink lines with a dry brush, dragging the ink out.

Rubbing Alcohol Gets Results

Catch spotted fever! Splash and sprinkle away with isopropyl alcohol for distinctive patterning.

Paint watercolors or dyes onto your paper of choice. Or use a thin wash of acrylic paint, as shown here on textured paper made for acrylics. While the paint is still damp, drop alcohol into it. That's it!

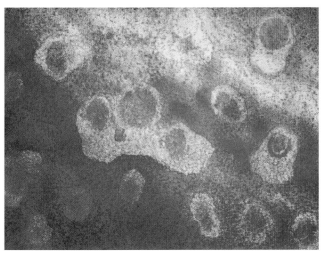

A scattering of droplets of 70 percent rubbing alcohol on damp watercolor washes sometimes results in this bull's-eye effect, also called "fish-eyes."

Try doing the same thing with mineral spirits, too. Such solvents tend to push the colorants aside. A brush loaded with acetone made these marks in very moist acrylic ink (on textured paper made for acrylics). When dry, the page was augmented with chalk pastels in a few places.

Smokin' Hot!

Apply carpenter's wood glue here and there to your paper of choice. This example began as a collage of tissue papers on brown Kraft paper. Lay the page on a non-flammable surface and (while the glue is still wet) add heat to the glued areas with a butane micro-torch. *Work outdoors or in a well-ventilated area and wear a respirator mask. Read and follow all precautions on the torch and butane packaging.*

Or you can create an entirely different effect with a heat gun instead of an iron. The Tyvek shrinks up in a dimensional manner when you do this, and the creases are permanent.

The wet glue should prevent the paper from catching on fire. Do not hold the flame too close to the paper or in one spot for too long. The glue will bubble, boil, and/or brown, resulting in very interesting effects.

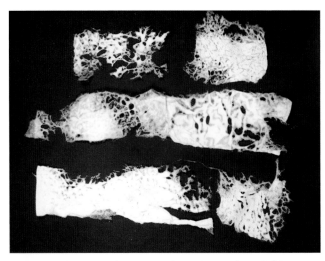

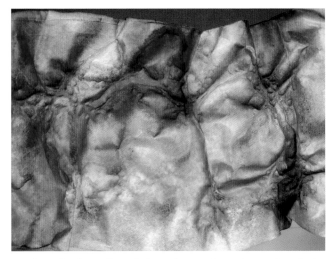

Washes of color will settle into the nooks and crannies nicely.

Here's another hot idea to try. Place pieces of Tyvek (the fibrous, strong stuff that some soft mailing envelopes are made of) on a Teflon pressing sheet. Cover with aluminum foil or another ironing sheet and press with a clothes iron at the polyester setting. With enough heat, some of the Tyvek will melt away, leaving a sort of paper lace behind.

Is It Cold in Here?

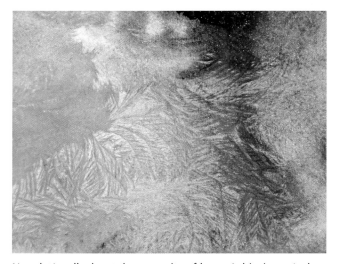

Now let's talk about the *opposite* of heat. Achieving a Jack Frost effect is tricky and very uncertain, but do give it a try. I suggest soaking watercolor paper first, adding very fluid paint, and immediately freezing the paper. With some luck, you'll get a beautiful ice crystal pattern. If you live in a very cold climate, weigh down the damp paper outdoors and quickly add the paint there. Leave it outdoors to freeze. Many variables may affect your results, so experiment a bit if you're not getting the effect you want.

Another example.

Blot Spots

Spots and vibrant blobs make brilliant surface decorations.

This effect lends an aged, shabby-chic appearance to paper. Apply acrylic color to a surface (note the turquoise layer showing at the edges in the photo) and let it dry. Next, paint another layer in a complementary or contrasting color. Let it sit for a minute or less. Sprinkle larger and smaller drops of water onto the surface.

After a minute, blot the surface with a smooth cloth, lifting off the top color and revealing the color beneath.

This painted paper is the first step in recreating a pitted, oxidized metal look. Allow the background colors to dry before proceeding.

Next, paint over the background colors with a deep brown. While the brown acrylic is still moist, flick water onto it.

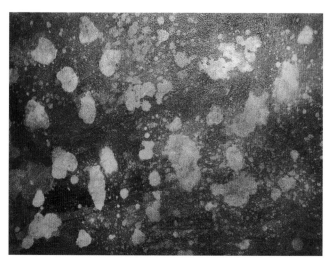

A grainy medium mixed with the acrylics aids in producing this corroded-looking, rusted metal effect.

See More Spots!

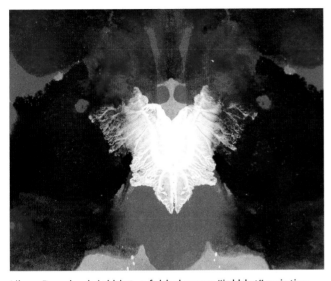

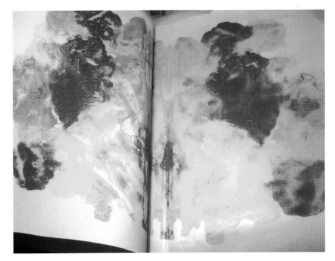

Like a Rorschach inkblot, a folded paper "inkblot" painting is likely to be symmetrical. Apply tempera, ink, or acrylic paint onto one half of a sheet of paper, then fold the paper and press the two sides together with the flat of your hand. In this instance, blobs of pearlescent gold liquid acrylic, black India ink, and red opaque drawing ink were placed on one side of folded red construction paper.

You can also use the butterfly method, placing drops of color into the center crease, folding the paper closed, and pushing the paint or ink away from the fold with your fingers.

Open the freezer paper and lay a clean sheet of paper onto the design. Run a brayer or a hand over the back of the paper. Peel it off and let it dry.

Drinking Straws and String

Just blow—or pull—for divine designs!

Drinking Straw Designs

And remember the monoprints we mentioned earlier? The folded freezer paper method is one of the most simple. Just paint several colors on the waxy side of the freezer paper, using any paint or ink. Fold the paper in half and press.

Branch out by blowing ink, liquid acrylic, or watercolors into organic lines resembling twigs or stems.

This abstract collage includes two pieces of brown paper on which India ink was blown into treelike shapes.

Pull That String!

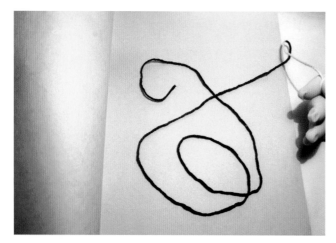

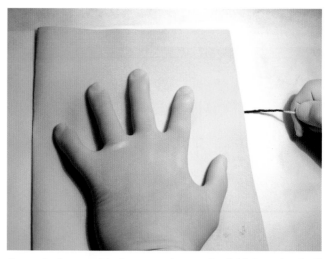

Cover the loops with the second paper (or fold the other half of the prefolded sheet over). Press and hold firmly with one hand. Grip the "tail" with the other hand and draw the string out steadily. Note that the fingers holding the papers flat should be spread wide.

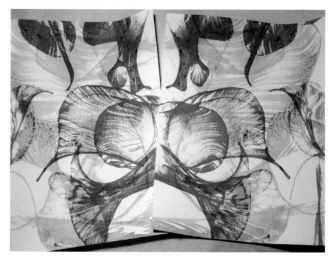

The pulled-string technique results in mirror images.

Cut a length of string about 1½ feet long. Immerse it in a shallow container of ink or liquid paint.

Wearing rubber gloves, pinch one end of the string and hold it up over the container. Run two fingers down the string to rid it of excess ink. Arrange the string in large loops on one sheet of paper (or on one half of a prefolded sheet). Leave a "tail" of string hanging off the edge.

Project: Jewelry Beads

There's something timeless about a string of beads; adornment has universal appeal. Fashioning beautiful paper beads for necklaces, bracelets, or earrings is enjoyable and rewarding!

TOOLS & MATERIALS

- Decorative papers, medium- to lightweight
- Scissors or paper-cutter
- Glue
- Bamboo skewer
- Jewelry wire, elastic, or cord
- Glass or wooden beads, jewelry findings, jewelry tools

Select papers. Light-colored and flowery ones produce a "Dresden china" effect, while dark reds, browns, and dull greens add a natural, earthy look.

Cut strips of paper about 1/2 to 1 inch wide and approximately 5 to 8 inches long, all the same size. (Later you might try a variety of widths and lengths to determine your favorite sizes.)

Narrow both sides of each strip to a point at one end, so that a long, tapered triangle results. The size and angle degree of the triangles determine the appearance of the finished bead. Make short, wide triangles if you want longer, thinner beads. Make long, narrow triangles for short, round beads.

Next, it's time to decide whether jewelry wire, cord, or elastic will be used in stringing the beads. Consult a jewelry-making book if you wish to learn how to use findings. This cuff bracelet was made with flexible cord and safety pins. You can add small metal, glass, shell, or wood beads and alternate them with the paper beads.

With the underside (the back) of the paper up, start at the broad end, and roll the paper tightly around a skewer. Keep the bead centered. Continue until nearly at the tip.

Put a small amount of glue on the point before finishing the rolling. Slip the bead from the skewer and spin it between your fingers to spread any excess glue over the surface. The result is a multicolored bead, larger in the center and tapering at both ends.

By varying the size and the amount of tapering of each paper "spear," you can produce different-shaped beads. They can also be painted if desired.

Coat each bead with gloss medium if you want a shiny finish. Place newly-varnished beads on waxed paper or freezer paper to dry.

Beads on ear wire.

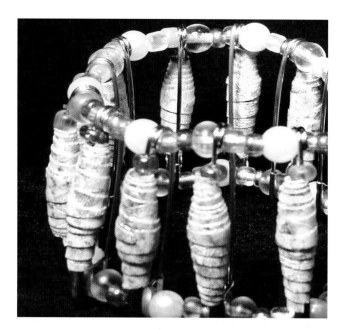

CHAPTER 7

Layering and Laminating

Translucent or opaque, torn or cut, the materials in
this section are the ingredients in artistic layer cakes!

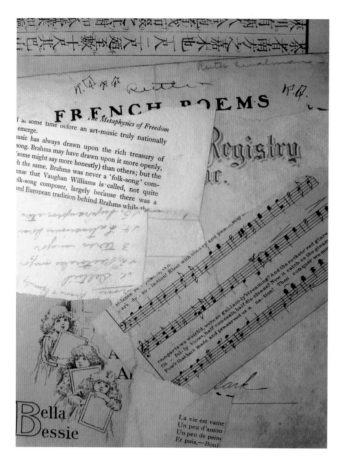

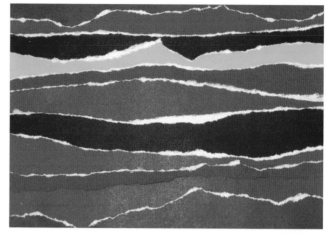

These glued-down strips were torn from art papers that were white on the back. The torn white edges add contrast and interest.

Here's a nearly effortless way to create an elegant page: Collage a layered assortment of aged, vintage papers onto a supporting sheet.

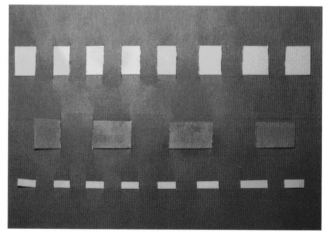

Children know that paper weaving can be fun and attractive. Cut slits in paper at rhythmic intervals and push colored strips through. The effects vary with color choice, the length and direction of the slits, and the spaces between them.

An office hole-punch and a larger craft punch made the positive and negative shapes in this design.

Even tape can adorn a page! Here, painter's tape, decorator's tape, masking tape, duct tape, and electrical tape were used.

Translucent Tissues

"Cellophanes" and sandwiching, overlays and inlays—these pages have all that and more.

Stained Glass

Place a page-sized piece of white tissue on waxed paper. Cut shapes from colored tissue papers and adhere them to the white tissue using fluid acrylic medium. To enhance transparency, cover the entire surface with gloss medium. When dry, flip the page over and gloss the back side. This technique is *clear*ly a winner!

Or tear pieces of tissue papers, mulberry papers, and more. Don't worry about wrinkles while gluing the papers together.

"Sandwiching"

Coating thin papers and layering them can be very effective. Try commercial tissues, Japanese papers, and one-ply from paper napkins.

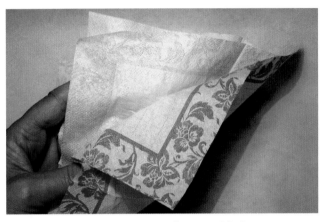

Remove all napkin layers except the one with the pattern.

Next, lay the receiving paper of choice (you can even use tissue or another printed napkin) onto waxed or freezer paper. Brush a coat of liquid acrylic medium all over it and press the second one-ply piece on top.

An additional coat of medium can be gently applied to the top and underside for more transparency. When it is dry, feel free to add paints, dyes, or inks wherever needed. I used a bit of acrylic paint to accent this finished decorative paper I made with two kinds of napkins.

TIP TALK

Colorful paper napkins can be purchased in countless patterns and designs. The best ones for this technique are those with a white or light-colored background.

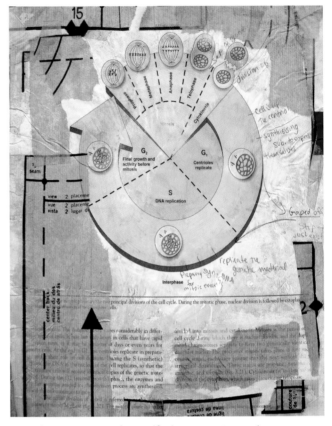

A sewing pattern or sheer gift tissue can top an image or text. Adhere it with liquid acrylic medium.

These dry, laminated leaf-print napkins leave something to be desired.

Alcohol inks applied judiciously added the final touch.

This old book page has been collaged with additional papers, but it can be improved.

The sewing pattern on top, made even more translucent with fluid acrylic medium, brings all the elements together very well.

This collage makes good use of dress pattern tissue.

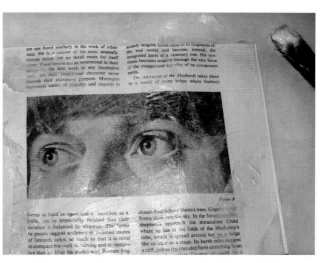

Here, a book page will receive several layers of crumpled tissues and ink.

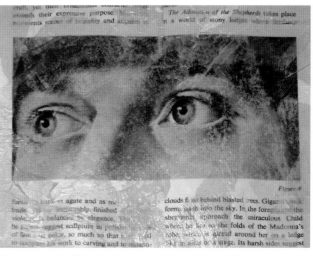

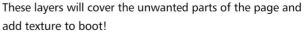

These layers will cover the unwanted parts of the page and add texture to boot!

The finished paper is shown here.

Waxed paper, ink, and cotton netting form the layers here.

Coating dried plant matter or insect wings with acrylic medium helps preserve them between translucent layers, even if inexpensive paper was used. Feathers can be encased between sheer papers, too.

Embedding

Try inserting small beads into gel medium or a thick pouring of liquid polymer medium. Sturdy paper is required as a base for this technique.

Here, portions of an unsuccessful watercolor painting were coated with liquid acrylic gloss medium. While it was still wet, two colors of 0.5-mm no-hole glass beads and ultrafine glitter were sprinkled into it

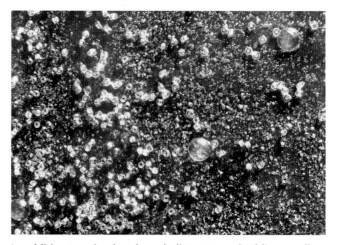

In addition to microbeads and glitter, try embedding small faux gems, as shown here. Or snip small lengths of metallic threads into acrylic medium. You can set in butterfly wings, too (when dry, add a topcoat of gloss medium).

Magazine Magic

Cut or tear images, patterns, textures, or colors from old magazines. Be sure to make smaller and larger shapes. Arrange them on a durable background page, overlapping or not. When the composition pleases you, glue down the pieces with gel medium.

Here I created a magazine collage in black and white.

Use the paint or ink of your choice to cover portions of the page, leaving other areas showing. Repeat with other colors as necessary. Paint ties the bits and pieces together and softens edges. In this example I toned and unified the page with sheer golden gesso and blue acrylic paint.

When dry, glaze the surface with a UV protectant, if desired. Acrylic UV Varnish provides a shield against dirt, grease, pollution, fading, and color shift.

Use your finished collage/paintings as they are, or as a background for more art. Another idea is to cut them apart to be used in other artwork.

Conjure up a striking page with a little paint and some recycled paper.

GOING GREEN

If you give your old magazines to others to read, good for you! You can use junk mail for this project instead.

Rumpled and Wrinkled

Textural effects are simple with tissue and more!

Tissue or Dryer Sheets

Crumple sheer tissue and adhere it to a heavier background paper with acrylic medium. Then flatten the bumps out with a brayer.

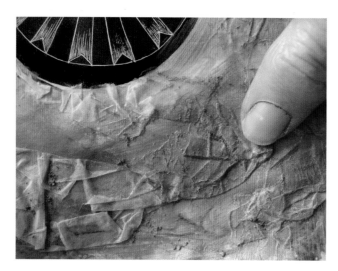

When the medium is dry, brush thin, dark paint into the crevices, wiping off the excess. To highlight with shimmer, rub loose, gleaming pigment (such as PearlEx or Perfect Pearls) onto the peaks. Or dry-brush the ridges with metallic paint.

Here is the completed page.

Another product that adds lots of texture to a page is the common softener sheet. Tear a used dryer sheet into pieces, or simply rip and poke holes in it. Apply it to a sturdy page using gel medium as an adhesive. Wrinkle it at will! Heavy-bodied acrylic paint will also hold down a dryer sheet. The finished page will have a rough, distressed look.

SMART ⟵⟶ SWAP

White craft glue diluted with water often works just as well as liquid acrylic medium.

Metal Deposit

Paper with a golden glow or silver shimmer can be dazzling. There's metallic paint, of course, but here's another way to make paper shine.

Store-bought, transfer-style metallic leafing sheets are simple to use, but there is a cheaper way. Gilding with recycled foils is smarter and greener! Save the gold and silver papers from chocolates. Case in point—an illustration page, colored with watercolors, will be embellished with thin foil wrappers.

Brush gel medium onto the paper and adhere a metallic scrap. Repeat with more foil pieces.

So faux, so good (sorry, I could not resist). In addition to fake foiling, try dry-brushing textured paper with a metallic powder/gel medium mixture. Dark papers work best to show off lustrous pearls or shiny metallics.

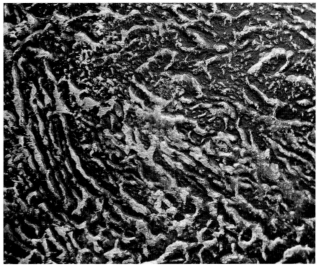

A second metallic color can be added after the first is dry.

Project: A Lucent Lampshade

Who wants a plain white shade or, worse, an old, stained one? Don't throw it away! Cover it and make it look fabulous. Beautifying a waste-basket with this method is easy, too.

TOOLS & MATERIALS

- Lampshade
- Kraft paper, wrapping paper, or freezer paper
- Translucent decorative papers
- Acrylic medium or other adhesive
- Wide brush
- Pencil
- Scissors
- Ruler
- Ribbon or art tape (optional)

Place the shade on its side on a very large sheet of brown or white paper. Beginning at the seam, trace with pencil along the top edge of the shade onto the paper, rolling the shade as you go to complete the rotation. It's best to angle the pencil toward the inside, since a slightly too-small template is better than one that is too tall. *Add* at least an inch past the seam, however, to be safe on the width.

Repeat for the bottom edge.

You'll create something like this. Enclose the shape with straight pencil lines at both ends.

To cover the shade, you can either decorate a very large piece of translucent paper or laminate several smaller pages together to create one sheet at least 12 by 24 inches for a medium-size shade, or larger for a big shade.

Cut out the Kraft paper pattern and test it on the shade. Remove any excess from the pattern, leaving just enough width for it to overlap itself by 1/2 inch to 3/4 inch at the seam. When you're sure the pattern is accurate, trace it onto the dry, decorative paper. Cut out the shape carefully.

Brush gel or liquid medium (or another fluid adhesive) onto the lampshade, working on about a 5-inch width at a time. Press the decorative paper flat with your hands from both inside and outside the shade. Continue applying adhesive and pressing the paper smoothly around the shade until done. This example uses napkin laminations.

If the shade is drum-style (straight up and down), you can glue ribbon trim or apply pretty tape to the top and bottom edges for a finished look. You can even cover the vertical seam if desired.

If the shade has a base that is wider than the top (like the coolie style you see here), consider using a strip of thin paper such as mulberry or tissue for the trim. It should be cut on the curve using your original pattern. This kind of trim has the advantage of being folded easily over the edges when adhered.

GOING GREEN

If you don't already have a lampshade in need of rejuvenation, find a low-cost one at thrift shop.

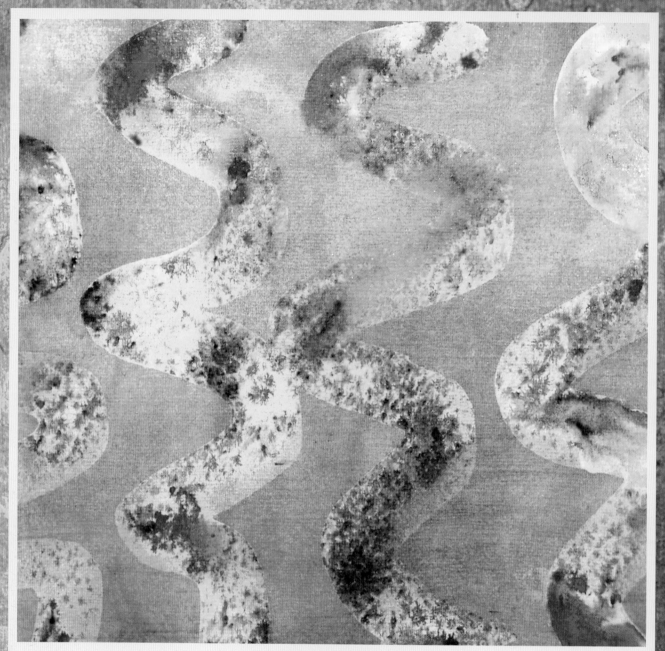

CHAPTER 8

Resists Get Results

In art lingo, a resist is a substance that prevents paint, ink, or dye from adhering to areas of a surface.

You can use resists to achieve many striking effects. Here are a variety of resist materials that protect paper from receiving paints, inks, or dyes.

GOING GREEN

The Elmer's Glue Crew Recycling Program saves used-up glue sticks and glue bottles from the landfill. Drop empties off at your local Walmart.

Varnish First!

Acrylic polymer varnish seals absorbent paper and, when dry, effectively resists another thin layer of paint, dye, or ink.

Polymer varnish (gloss) was applied to permeable prepainted paper and allowed to dry thoroughly. Then acrylic washes were added.

Gesso Resist

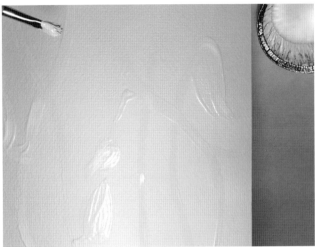

White or colored gesso stands firmly, in more ways than one! Squirt, drip, stamp, or paint it onto heavy, absorbent (not glossy) paper, and let dry thoroughly.

Then paint over the entire page with acrylics. Spritz immediately with water and wipe away the paint. The gessoed strokes or areas will be much lighter. If the gesso was thick, the design will be slightly raised, too.

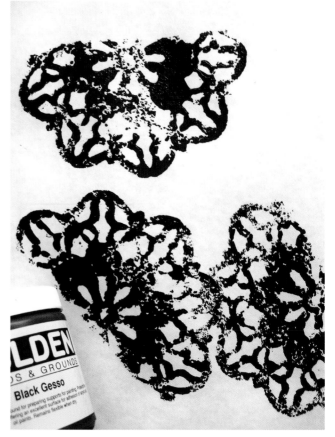

The lines at left were made with white gesso on 110-pound Canson acrylic paper. The thinner, clear gesso at right did not perform as well.

Gesso also comes in black (stamped onto cardstock here with a die-cut felt coaster), but you can mix acrylic paint in whatever color you wish with white gesso, too!

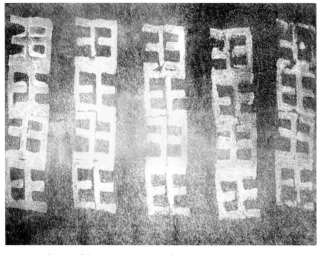

Stamped-on white gesso resisted paint on this white cardstock.

Detail of the same example, with much of the painted layer rubbed off.

Peeling with Petroleum Jelly

This method produces an interesting distressed, flaked-paint appearance.

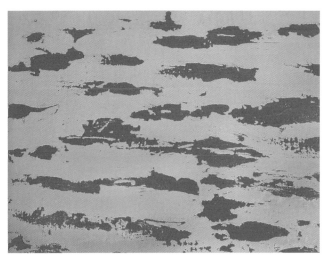

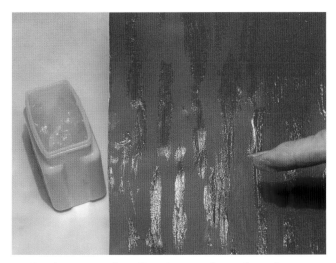

Apply a base coat of acrylic paint to a sheet of sturdy paper. Let dry.

Then use a rag, brush, or finger to streak on long blobs of petroleum jelly here and there, in one direction only. Don't cover the entire page!

When the page is dry, if you're not pleased with the results, you could apply petroleum jelly again and follow the same procedure as before with a third paint color.

Hair Gel Resist

Similar in effect to petroleum jelly, thick hair gel also withstands moderate overpainting. Buy an inexpensive kind of hair gel at a dollar store.

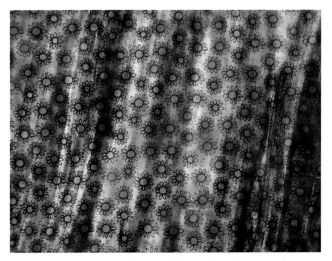

Gently paint the surface with a contrasting color of acrylic paint. Try to avoid dragging the petroleum jelly about too much when you do this. Allow the paint to dry thoroughly again.

Next, wash the page down with soapy water, rubbing gently to remove the petroleum jelly. Rinse and set aside on newspapers. When the page has dried, wipe any remaining residue off with a paper towel. (If the decorative sheet is too fragile to withstand a washing, use the wiping method only.)

A scrapbook paper was first washed with red watercolor. When the paint was dry, hair gel stripes were brushed on. (You can also cover a printing block with hair gel and stamp it onto paper.)

A wash of dark green liquid acrylic was added over the whole thing. When that was dry, the hair gel was wiped off.

More Resist Media and Effects

A wash of red dye beads up on the wax.

Wax crayons or china markers (the kind with the peel-off wrappers) present an easy way to resist water-based paint. Marks made by paraffin, white candle wax, or white crayon seem to disappear on paper until they are painted over. The examples shown here were done with white crayon on drawing paper.

You can also use colored crayons, oil sticks, or regular oil pastels. Apply them quite heavily so they will repel paint well. Wet absorbent paper before adding dye or thin paint if a smooth result is desired. The wash of paint should be done in a contrasting color.

For the paper pictured here, I drew on a dry, painted sheet of watercolor paper with a yellow Shiva oil stick. Then I applied thin acrylic ink over it.

Dorland's is another waxy medium that resists paint. Let it dry on the paper before painting over it.

TIP TALK

To monitor the progress of a design you're making with white wax, hold the paper at an angle to a light source to see the nearly invisible marks.

Colorful magazine pages (choose ones that aren't too dark) can be doodled on with paraffin or white candle wax and covered with a wash of fluid acrylic. Here, a thin coat of dark brown was gently applied to a magazine page. Don't scrub as you paint!

Yes, thin magazine papers will pucker; wait until they are dry, then flatten them with a heavy book.

Here, crayon shavings (on a sheet of scrapbooking paper) were covered with a piece of scratch paper and melted. (To melt, put several cover sheets on top and use a heat gun or a clothes iron.) The crayon spots in this example resisted a later wash of walnut ink.

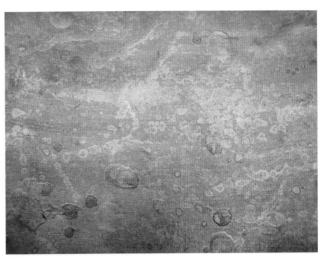

Aquawax is another resist medium which can be used in several different ways. Shake the container well and use it at room temperature, straight from the bottle. Apply it with a brush, a sponge, or a stamp. (In this instance, the medium was mixed with metallic gold powder before it was splattered onto the paper.)

Let it dry thoroughly before washing over the surface with any thin, water-based paint. Use a rag to wipe excess paint off if necessary.

You can create a superb colorful effect by first painting strokes of full-strength Aquawax with a brush. While it's still wet, sprinkle Brusho powdered pigment into it. Always wash Aquawax out of brushes immediately after use.

Dry the paper flat. Then apply a wash over all. Spritz with water if the paint coverage is too dense.

Micro Glaze is a clear waxy paste product that resists liquids well, too. Even neutral shoe polish or Johnson's Paste Wax will work.

Rubber Is Ducky

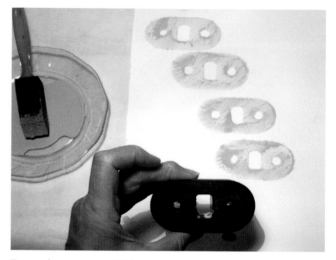

Two points to note: Frisket can damage soft papers (such as the watercolor paper used here) upon removal, especially if left on the surface for a long time. Also, the latex in masking fluid may cause allergic reactions!

Liquid frisket, also called art masking fluid, is a rubbery material which can be dripped, dribbled, painted, or stamped wherever one wishes to preserve an area. There is also a Masquepen on the market which allows the user to draw thin lines with masking fluid.

In the project pictured above, I covered the white of the paper with branching lines and dots of masking fluid. Later, I painted watercolors over them. When the paint was dry, I rubbed the frisket away, leaving white stems.

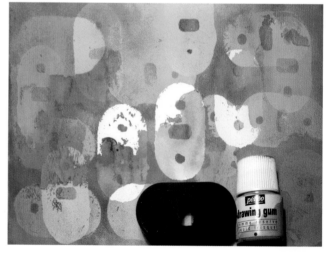

Frisket fluid was removed in some places and added in others before each new layer of paint was applied to this design.

SMART ←→ SWAP

Rubber cement works as a resist like frisket. However, consumer-grade rubber cement may deteriorate paper over time if it is not acid-free. Also, avoid breathing in large amounts of the fumes.

Shake the bottle of frisket well before using, and apply it to dry surfaces only. It does clog up brush bristles, so use cheap, old brushes with it. Here, masking fluid in a shallow container is applied to a found rubber object with a wide foam brush.

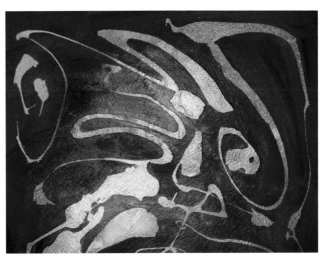

Roll off the rubber cement with a rubber cement pickup tool or with your thumb.

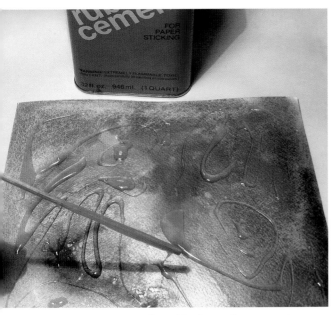

Acrylic paints were painted on this sheet of paper and allowed to dry before rubber cement was dribbled on with a bamboo skewer.

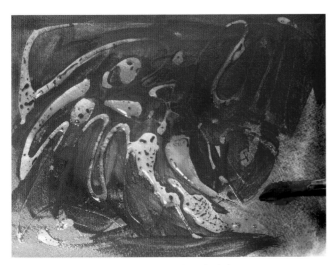

Another layer of acrylic is brushed on lightly.

This finished rubber cement resist example was enhanced with a few marker lines.

Glue Factory

Washable school glue gel works wonders on some papers. I recommend watercolor paper or paper made for acrylics.

Squeeze out glue lines, shapes, or dots on dry white or colored paper, or apply with a brush or stamp.

In this case, I altered a child's foam stamp. Let the glue dry.

There are also many fabric wash-out resists on the market that produce similar results. Colored fabric resist products can be permanent.

The end result.

Next, paint over it with thin acrylic or staining dyes or watercolor. Let dry. Later, gentle rubbing under a warm-water faucet washes out the glue.

Repeat the entire process with more glue and other colors if desired.

A Permanent Solution

Permanent fabric glue was squeezed onto commercial scrapbook paper. When dry, it was painted over with a wash of brown.

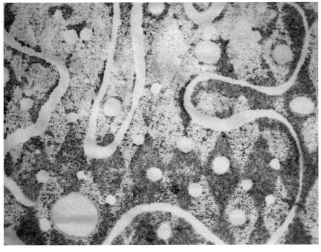

The back of the same page has plenty of appeal. Always check the backside of paper you decorate—you might like it better than the front!

Here's another kind of glue resist—this one requires permanent craft glue, not the washable variety. Use white glue that dries quite clear. Select a full magazine page to alter—one with colors or visual textures you like. Don't worry about images, since they might be eradicated later. Given that you will be lightening the page, avoid pages with lots of white.

Squeeze out dots, shapes, and lines of glue wherever you wish to preserve a color or pattern on the page. Let it dry.

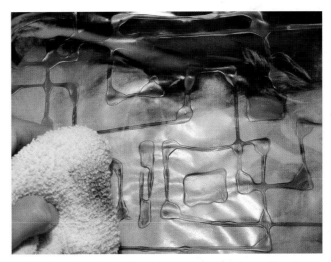

Use a mineral spirits solvent on a rag in a well-ventilated room. Wear rubber gloves. Scour the dry page, rubbing with the rag repeatedly until the exposed magazine inks fade. They will nearly disappear with enough elbow grease. Use care around the dried glue bits, or they might pop off.

When one part of the cloth becomes saturated with ink, switch to a cleaner portion.

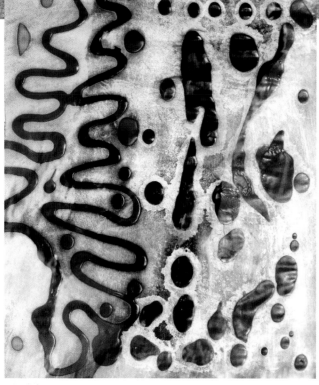

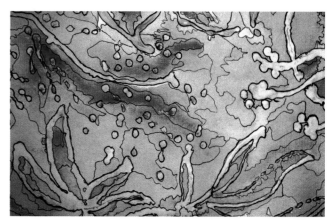

The finished page.

This lovely floral, which uses another method entirely, takes some time to create. Flower, stem, and leaf lines are squeezed onto watercolor paper with Elmer's craft glue. Since tar gel dries completely clear, you can substitute it for the craft glue if you wish. Hold a spoonful of clear tar gel high over a sheet of watercolor paper and drizzle lines onto the paper.

When the glue or tar gel is dry, wet the paper with clear water and paint it with watercolors. The paint will bleed and spread in interesting ways.

Instead of applying glue to a single page, try using one page as a background for smaller magazine pieces that you've glued onto it, collage-style. *Then* add glue lines and shapes and proceed as described.

After the watercolor is dry, outline every contour with an ultra-fine marker. Define each edge of every single shape. Instead of a black fine-line marker, you could try a metallic pen—copper, silver, or gold—for a rich, elegant look.

Project: Covering a Mat or Frame

Cover faded mats or unsightly frames with pretty papers that complement what they enclose. You can use the same process to customize a dimensional alphabet letter or decorate a plain switch-plate cover or outlet cover to match a room's décor.

Covering a Rectangular Mat

Photo and art mats are simple to cover because they are flat.

Lay the mat onto the back side of the decorative paper. Lightly trace the inside opening and the outside edge of the mat. Set the mat aside.

With pencil and ruler, draw an X corner to corner (diagonally) inside the inner opening.

Next, measure 1/2 inch outward from all the outside edges of the mat and draw a straight border there. Cut around this rectangle, creating a neat edge on the outside. (Later this 1/2-inch border will be wrapped around to the back of the mat.)

At the outer corners, draw straight lines at a 45-degree angle, as shown (illustrated here as dotted lines).

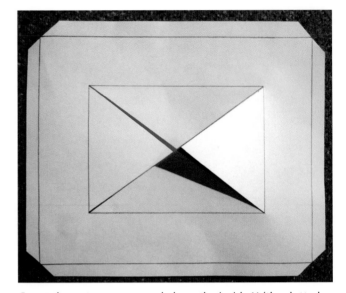

Cut at the outer corners and along the inside X (the dotted lines in the diagram). When that's done, turn the paper to the decorative side. Score and crease along the solid lines of the template.

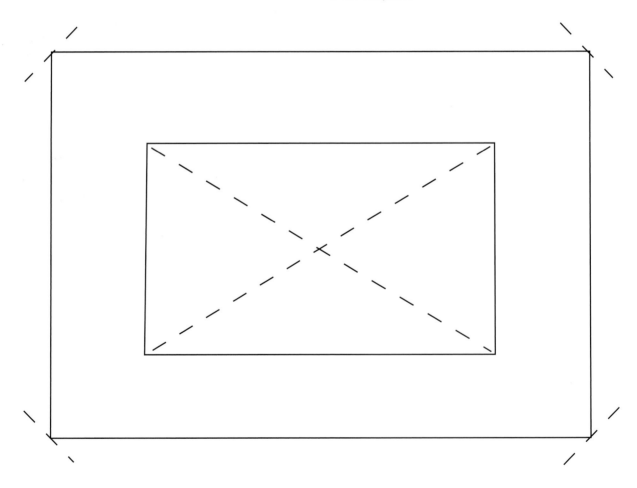

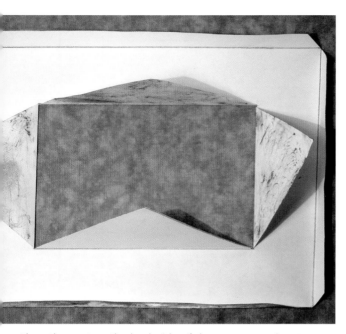

Covering a Simple Wooden Frame

Place the mat on the back side of the paper covering to verify fit. The points of the X (the picture opening) will likely need to be trimmed, as shown here.

Place the mat on newspaper or freezer paper and apply a thin coat of adhesive to it. Immediately press the mat into place on the back of the decorative paper. Flip it over and smooth out any wrinkles. Turn to the back once again and adhere the outer edge flaps to the back of the mat.

Papers may shrink as they dry, warping the mat, so put a piece of waxed paper over it and heavy books or pressing boards on top. Let dry overnight.

Make personalized picture frames for friends and family using original papers and common craft supplies. A handcrafted gift like this will be used and appreciated.

Choose either an unfinished wooden picture frame or a battered, shabby one. Remove the glass and backing, if they are present, from the back of the frame. Sand the frame lightly, particularly if it has a finish. Varnished frames should be roughened up a bit so they accept the adhesive more thoroughly.

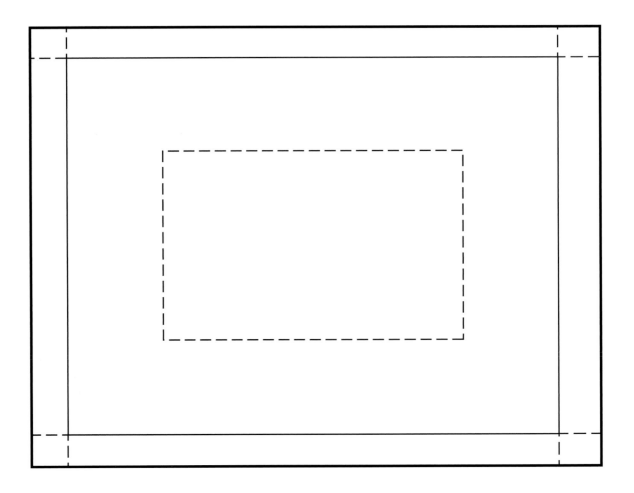

Select a large, decorated page, bigger on all sides than the frame and its depth combined. Turn the decorative paper upside down and place the frame onto the paper with the frame's front side down. With a pencil, lightly trace the photo opening onto the paper, shown in this diagram as a dotted line. Also trace the outer edge of the frame, and use the ruler to extend those lines beyond the frame (shown as dotted lines at each corner).

Remove the frame from the paper and measure its depth to determine the outer boundary for the decorative paper (shown as a bold line in the diagram). Draw that rectangle onto the paper with ruler and pencil. Cut along that outer line to remove excess paper.

Using scissors or a craft knife, carefully cut out the photo opening and the four outside corner squares (all the dotted lines). Test the paper on the frame to see if it will be a good fit. Trim any excess. Set the paper aside.

Place the frame on a sheet of newspaper. Paint the inside rim of the frame in a coordinating color and let it dry.

On the "good" (decorative) side of the paper, score and crease along the line representing the frame edge (the solid line on the diagram). Apply a thin coat of adhesive to the frame—Mod Podge or gel medium will do nicely—and glue the covering to the frame front and sides. While the adhesive is still wet, smooth out the entire surface. Keep flattening the paper with your hands until you are quite sure there will be no wrinkles or curled-up edges.

When the glue under the paper is thoroughly dry, add a sealer over all if desired. Embellishments, if any, should be attached last. Consider the subject of the photo when selecting these: Seashells are perfect for a beach scene, varnished dog biscuits for a pet photo. Other potential decorative items include buttons, ribbons, rhinestones, chipboard letters, and more. Glue dots or other strong adhesive should be used to attach embellishments. You can also attach harmonizing paper shapes that have either been torn or cut with decorative paper punches or edging scissors.

CHAPTER 9

Solvents and Spirits

You can make arty, imaginative papers with latex paint
and common household cleaners—how convenient!

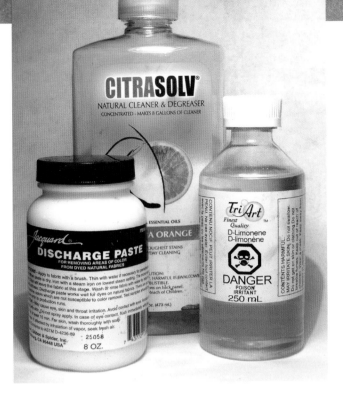

The Pressure's On

Here's another way to use Citra Solv—the results can be out of this world! You can expect fantastic patterns and surreal images with this stuff, although the outcomes will vary.

Wipeout!

Removing unwanted text or a company logo is easy. Tear out a full magazine page with photographs. Select colors, visual textures, or shapes that appeal to you, and others that you want to remove. Use rubber gloves and protect the work surface.

Pour full-strength Citra Solv generously into a rag and scrub areas of the magazine page gently until they fade. Be selective, washing out lettering or anything you wish to blanch all but completely.

Citra Solv is a natural, biodegradable product with a very strong citrus scent. In addition to the orange-scented product, the company now makes a pleasant, lavender-scented one.

A cotton swab coated with Citra Solv can be used to create clouds, waterfalls, and more.

This method of making decorative paper leaves a lot to chance. Choose an old magazine such as National Geographic with lots of photo pages. Vivid, richly colored magazine photos will likely produce the best results.

Working atop plenty of old newspapers, go through the magazine and saturate all the photo pages with Citra Solv. Apply it liberally to both sides of each page with a large brush or a spritzer bottle.

Close up the magazine, press down hard on the cover, and cover it with freezer paper or plastic wrap. Lay a heavy book on top and let it sit for no more than twenty-five minutes.

Do not allow the pages to dry or they will stick together. Pull the wet pages apart by the corners, set them onto newspapers, and let dry overnight. The scent can be overpowering if there are many pages, so you may want to put them in a garage or other out-of-the-way place to dry.

Your first attempt will be experimental and you may have some disappointing pages. Keep trying, as the successes are really worth it! Conduct experiments by changing the amounts, times, and types of magazines you use.

This simple landscape collage was made by tearing Citra Solv papers and adhering them to a support, although cutting the pieces, mosaic-style, is another option.

Paint back into the papers if desired, or draw with gel pens or other drawing tools.

Lighten Up

Color can be leached with laundry bleach. The example above was done on brown construction paper; you could enhance this design with extra color if desired.

Bleach is to be used with caution, and only on papers that are not destined for use in serious fine art pieces. Chlorine bleach is alkaline and may cause the paper fibers to weaken.

Dip a cotton swab into liquid bleach, or use a bleach gel pen. Papers react differently, so try several types. The bleach can be rinsed off the paper after it has done its work.

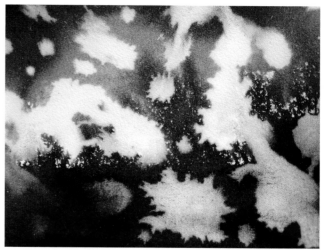

This sheet of watercolor paper was colored with fabric dye. Liquid laundry bleach was applied while the paper was still damp.

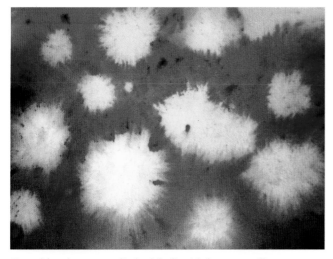

Here, bleach was applied while liquid dye was still wet.

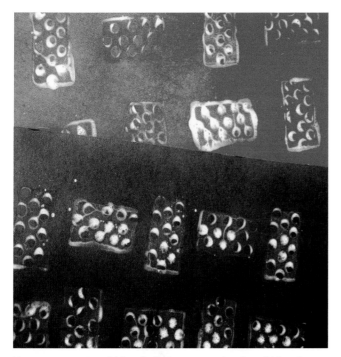

You can stamp and bleach designs, too. Apply gel bleach to the stamp and press onto paper.

Get Your Discharge Papers Here

Discharge paste is a product for removing areas of color from dyed fabrics, but it works on absorbent paper too. Here, it's applied with a brush to a sheet of construction paper.

When the discharge paste is dry, steam iron the paper at a low setting—the more steam, the better. No cover sheet is necessary. Magic happens!

It's not necessary to rinse the page to wash out the discharge paste.

Project: Create a Collage

A collage is a work of art composed by pasting various materials on one surface. Producing a two-dimensional, mixed media piece with decorated papers is fun and easy.

TOOLS & MATERIALS

- Canvas panel, illustration board, or other sturdy support
- Gel medium and/or other adhesive
- Paints and inks of choice
- Brushes
- Drawing tools (optional)
- Scissors (optional)
- A variety of decorative papers
- Imagery (photographs, photocopies, prints)
- Ephemera, text, and fairly flat objects

Choose a central theme for this project. Perhaps it can represent someone you know—their favorite colors, hobbies, music, foods, anything!

Select a pleasing color scheme and assemble a number of harmonious collage materials of varying textures. Traditionally, collages are made of materials such as scraps of paper and other flat media: newspaper and magazine clippings, photographs, maps, diagrams, and wallpaper. You can also use other materials: string, feathers, textiles—the possibilities are endless.

Cut or tear potential background pieces and arrange them on the substrate without glue. Work forward by layering on more (and smaller) elements without adhering them. Allow portions of the background materials to show beneath the others.

Use both repetition and variety in designing your collage. Balance larger and smaller shapes and be sure to add a focal point (a main point of interest). When you have found a pleasing composition, sketch or photograph it before removing the pieces from the base.

Adhere the background papers first. (Some artists paint the canvas panel first, and let that dry beforehand.) Apply gel medium or glue to each piece in turn and firmly press it down. Rub it flat from the center to the edges. If a smooth surface is desired, allow each to dry flat before gluing other materials on top (although puckered, wrinkled paper can be very interesting).

Experiment as you add more elements. Tear or cut paper or fabric shapes and don't be afraid to move the components around as necessary. Insert, remove, and rearrange. Be flexible and deviate from the original sketch as needed.

Consider adding texture with flat buttons or beads, fibers, small seashells, lace, or such. Avoid too much clutter, however.

Add the finishing touches. Tie the various pieces together by brushing on paint here and there, or by drawing, stamping, or stenciling. You have infinite options with collage, so experiment with your own methods.

Acrylic paint unifies the piece and disguises some edges. Allow to dry thoroughly. Then, if desired, seal the surface by brushing on gloss or matte varnish.

THE PRINCIPLES OF ART

In planning an artwork, use the elements of art—color and value, line, shape, form, and texture—to their best advantage.

In addition to the two concepts I've already mentioned (balance and variety), consider other principles of art as you work. Rhythm is a visual "beat," a regular pattern of color, line, shape, or form. Emphasis occurs when part of the page stands out, drawing the viewer's eye. Without it, a piece may seem boring. However, when all the elements of a page combine to make a harmonious, complete whole, unity occurs.

CHAPTER 10

Just Faux Fun

Amazing effects can be found in a can or a jar—
webbing aerosols and sprays that produce hammered metal,
suede, and stone effects, art products that create the
look of stone or the texture and sheen of iron.

Faux-finished papers (above) and a few of the many faux finishes available.

Dark tissue shows off white webbing nicely.

Pretend Patina

For a faux metal verdigris (a patina of blue-green), first paint metallic copper acrylic or spray paint on a page. Metallic gold paint works, too!

While the paint is still tacky, brush on a commercial copper patina solution. This page, from a book on Celtic art, has also been colored and drawn on.

Ersatz Encaustic

Love the thick, rich look of melted and polished beeswax on an artwork? Want to save time and expense while avoiding the issue of hot wax? Here's a layering process with acrylic media that imitates the effect!

Choose rigid paper for this technique. If it has been pre-painted, allow it to dry first.

Then use about 1/2 cup semigloss or matte self-leveling acrylic medium (or gel medium mixed with two tablespoons water). Add a very small amount of pale yellow or off-white acrylic paint to simulate the color of beeswax.

Spread the mixture generously onto the paper with a wide, flat brush or painting knife. Allow it to dry thoroughly, probably overnight.

Next, add a translucent painted or drawn design. Be sure to use permanent, waterproof ink or paint. Colors with translucence include alizarin crimson, the pthalos, and the quinacridones. Let dry.

Finally, another layer of the faux wax mixture adds just the right touch.

An easy variation that *does* use wax calls for a food-warming tray or pad. The Icarus Drawing Board, a product for artists, also plugs in and has a warming side. Lay paper on the warm tray and "paint" it with ordinary wax crayons. Use a white crayon or a chunk of paraffin to blend other colors or create sheer areas.

In this example, white paper was made more translucent with a piece of paraffin and three crayons. White candle wax can also be used as a blending tool in this method.

Fake Fresco

Give paper an old-world, European feeling with this aged-plaster technique.

To create an old Italian look lush with texture, first spread a fairly thin coat of flexible modeling or molding paste, joint compound, or thick gesso on sturdy paper. (Ready-made stuccolike art products exist, as well.)

Add in a little gold, cream, or tan acrylic paint. Use a painting knife to create a troweled texture on the surface. Let dry. The paper should not be bent after this, or the surface might chip off in places. Then again, that could yield an interesting effect!

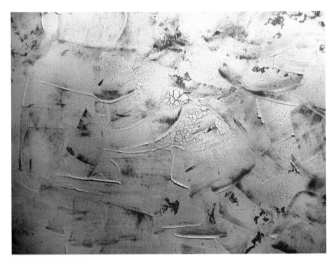

This distressed plaster effect was created in a different manner: Rigid paper was first covered with rosy paint. Then a very thin coat of crackle medium was applied to the paper with a trowel.

The DecoArt line of Texture Crackle medium is available in a variety of colors. They also make a Terra Cotta product with warm, earthy tones.

Glaze the dry, textured surface with one or several warm colors of acrylic (choose from burnt umber, burnt sienna, raw sienna, or yellow ochre) mixed with matte medium. It's important to seal porous materials before the next step, and acrylic medium does this. It prevents a stain from soaking right in later.

Yet another way to fake a plaster effect is to use a store-bought paper medium, as shown here. It's a ready-to-use, thick paint with actual paper fibers that produce the look of handmade paper. Apply a thin, spotty coat to sturdy paper with a sponge or a painting knife.

When the glaze is dry, "antique" the page for even more contrast. Apply thin, dark acrylic or ink. Immediately wipe off the surface with a cotton cloth, using a circular motion.

When the glue is dry, smear on some brown paste-wax shoe polish. Work in a well-ventilated area, wiping off the excess with a soft cloth. The odor will dissipate after several hours.

Pale yellow paper pulp on an old file folder page was allowed to dry and was then painted with a wash.

Mock Leather

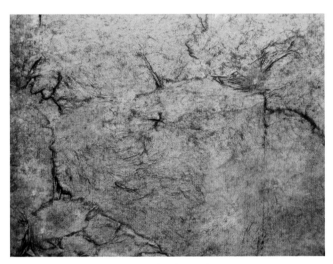

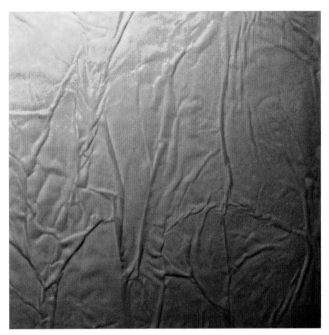

Although I prefer the results of the previous method, there is another way to make fake leather. Crumple thin tissue paper, open it flat, and set it aside. Spread craft glue or acrylic medium onto a base paper such as cardstock. Tap the sheet of tissue down into the glue. Allow it to dry.

Here are two ways to mimic leather using paper.

The first calls for an ordinary paper bag (or brown Kraft paper). Tear it into irregular pieces, crumple them, and smooth them out again. Glue them onto a base sheet of paper, overlapping the pieces to cover the surface completely. Smooth out any bubbles with your hands, and make sure that the edges are adhered well.

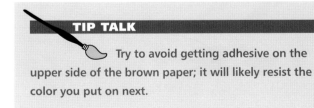

TIP TALK

Try to avoid getting adhesive on the upper side of the brown paper; it will likely resist the color you put on next.

Next, mix up a glaze of semi-gloss acrylic medium of brown umber, burnt umber, or any leatherlike colors. Paint the page. Add "stitching" with a marker if desired.

Imitation Marble

Marbled designs are printed patterns (of ink suspended atop a solution) that are transferred to paper or fabric. Several marbling methods exist. The techniques below are much simpler than those that are hundreds of years old! I'll show you how to marble without mordant or sizing.

E-Z Marbling

This approach is my favorite marbling method, and it is *so* simple!

Cardstock works well for this method, but try marbling other papers, too.

Cover the work surface. Fill the bottom of a large, shallow pan with aerosol shaving cream. Smooth the surface with a squeegee or other tool—I use a five-inch-wide taping knife. Drop two or three different colored inks onto the surface here and there. I suggest liquid dye, walnut ink, or alcohol ink. Experiment to discover which ones you like best.

Now connect the dots. Comb into them with a toothpick, hair pick, fork, or stir-stick to make an interesting pattern. Know when to stop, so you don't over-mix the colors.

Hold a sheet of paper (cut to fit the tray) by two diagonal corners and press it firmly into the surface. Smooth out any air bubbles with your fingertips.

After about a minute, lift the paper carefully from the pan and lay it face-up on newspaper.

Now either wipe the shaving cream off the page or rinse it off under the tap. Allow the paper to dry flat on newsprint, or hang it to dry.

It may be possible to marbleize another sheet of paper with the same shaving cream and design. Or you can scrape off the top layer of colored shaving cream and repeat with more swirled drops.

If you used alcohol inks or walnut inks, it's safe to wash the used-up shaving cream down the drain.

TIP TALK

While many artists pre-treat paper with a coating to "grab" the paint better, some of us find it time-consuming and unnecessary. None of the marbled papers here have been pre-treated.

An alcohol ink and two colors of walnut inks were used to create these pages. All three pieces of cardstock shown here were printed from the same batch.

Marbling is unpredictable, so practice lots!

Marbling with Ink on Water

This ancient Japanese technique of decorating paper with inks is believed to be the oldest form of marbling, originating in China over 2,000 years ago. Inks dropped carefully will float on a still water surface. Then gentle blowing across them causes swirls to form.

This delicate process can result in understated, natural-looking patterns on paper, depending on several variables. Outcomes will fluctuate, so carry out some trials. You'll need at least two fine brushes.

Wear protective clothing and cover the work surface. Put an inch or two of water in the pan. Prepare the ink or dye mixture in a small container by mixing 1 teaspoon ink or dye with 1 teaspoon water and 1 drop of PhotoFlo (or Jet Dry, a product used in dishwashers). PhotoFlo is a film rinse agent used in photography. In another small container—and with a different fine brush—mix 1 teaspoon water with 1 drop of the chosen surfactant (rinse agent). The ratios given here are not infallible, so experiment with the proportions.

Barely touch the tip of the fine brush you used to mix the ink into the prepared ink and then gently onto the water's surface. Break up the color film floating on the surface with a very light touch of the tip of the second brush with the surfactant solution, right in the center of the color. Repeat with other colors if desired, alternating color and rinse agent solutions.

Create a few swirls in the floating ink by blowing gently on the surface or by dragging a very fine tool through it. Hold a sheet of paper (cut to fit the tray) by diagonal corners, curve it, and drop it onto the surface center-first. Lift the paper from water and let dry on newspapers or freezer paper, or hang to dry.

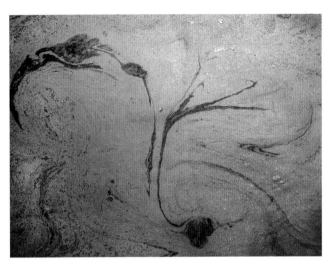

Subtle coloring is common with this method. Some of the inks in this example were shimmering metallics.

The water will become "muddy" after several prints, so lay a sheet of newspaper on the water to pick up the inks. You can also skim the surface with newspaper, picking up unwanted bits.

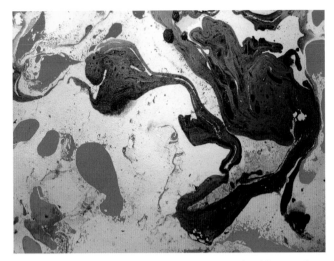

Oil paints, thinned with turpentine or mineral spirits, can be used instead of ink or dye. Swirl the droplets in the pan of water with a toothpick or bamboo skewer.

Oil-based (not latex) spray paints can be used, too! Simply point the can toward the water and spray. If you use spray paints, do it outdoors or in an area with good ventilation. Quickly, before the paint sets, swirl it and marbleize your paper. This very bright example was made with brilliant spray paint floating on water.

More Marbleizing Techniques

Pearly powders, wallpaper paste, and other thickening agents can be used to replicate marble, too.

Pour the paste into a large, shallow pan. If using liquid acrylic paints, thin them with water until runny. Drop three to four colors onto the surface of the wallpaper paste.

Swirl the colors with spiral, zigzag, or arch motions. Note the homemade "rake" used here: It's made from toothpicks and tape.

To use the wallpaper paste method, combine 1/3 cup of wallpaper paste powder with about 2 quarts of cold water, whisking well. When the mixture is free of lumps, let it sit an hour to thicken, stirring every fifteen minutes. The mixture will be soupy.

Hold a sheet of paper (cut to fit the tray) by diagonal corners and drop it onto the surface. Press out any air bubbles gently. Let the paper float for a short time to absorb the color. Lift paper and let dry on newspapers or freezer paper, or hang to dry.

Excess paint may settle to the bottom of the pan. The same paste solution can be used several times, and it can be stored in a lidded jar in the refrigerator for a week. Don't discard excess paint down the drain but rather wipe it out of the pan.

This next technique is pan-free! Mix up a creamy paint made of PearlEx or other mica powder and water. This method yields lustrous pages, but it works best with less absorbent cardstock or glossy paper.

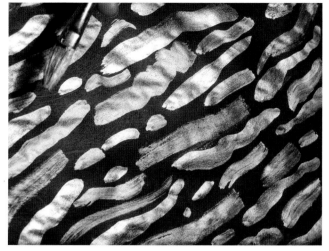

First, prepare several small batches of harmonious colors of pearly powder pastes. Brush squiggles and streaks onto dark paper, as shown.

I like this simulated marble effect just as it is, but you can crumple up a paper towel and dab in places if you wish a smoother effect.

Spritz with water and tilt the paper to cause some running.

Get Crackling In No Time!

You can buy many different types of crackle paints and mediums. Even spray-on crackle paint is available!

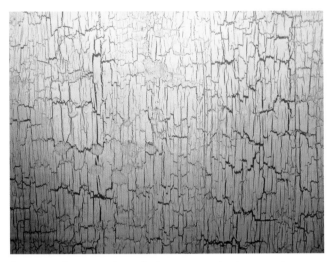

Some products require painting a second color over the crackle medium—be sure to use a much lighter or darker one.

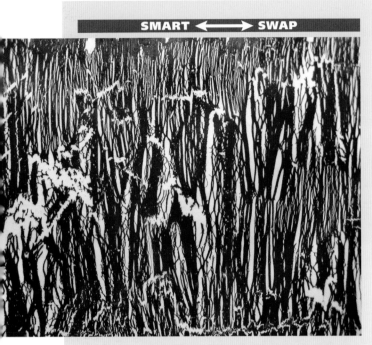

SMART ⟷ SWAP

You can trade expensive crackle paints for ordinary white Elmer's craft glue. Apply glue to a dry, colored surface and, while it's still tacky, paint over it with thin acrylic. Several hours later the fissures will be fantastic!

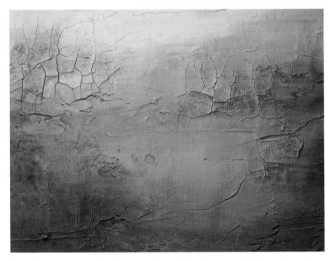

Crackle paste products require a sturdy support. The heavier the application, the larger the clefts. You'll find more delicate cracks where the paste is thin. A dark wash rubbed into the crevices accentuates them.

Project: 3-D Art

Create a dimensional collection of memories in a meaningful grouping, or create a freestanding mixed-media piece with a message.

Before gathering the materials for this altered art piece, select a theme, motif, and/or color scheme. The piece pictured is based on the myth of Icarus.

TOOLS & MATERIALS

- Shallow metal or wooden box (or other container)
- Ephemera, images, fabrics, and dimensional objects
- Adhesives of choice
- Painted papers
- Acrylic paints, mediums, and assorted brushes
- Water in containers
- Rags or paper towels
- Scissors or craft knife

Select a "frame" that will hold the elements (materials) to be included. A shadowbox or cigar box might be ideal. You can gesso it in advance if the vessel is unsightly or extremely porous, although the use of papers and acrylic medium may make gesso unnecessary.

Choose coordinating decorated papers that complement the selected images, fabrics, or objects. Consider a mix of opaque, translucent, and textured materials.

You might wish to paint the vessel before proceeding. If so, a coat of gesso beforehand may help the paint adhere. You can also alter some of the parts before you put everything together. For example, the "invisible man" pictured here will be given a different head!

When the found objects and other elements are ready, arrange them, working from back to front. Don't glue anything down yet!

When you have an arrangement you're happy with, make a sketch or take a photo before removing the top (or front) pieces. Cut or tear papers to fit the background and the frame, inside and out.

You can cover the entire container or leave some of the original box bare. Brush a thin coat of acrylic gel on the backs of the papers and on the container. Smooth out bubbles and excess glue from the adhered papers.

Then begin attaching the dimensional items, working from the back (or bottom) first. A good, strong adhesive for heavy objects is E6000. Heavy gel medium will secure medium-weight or lighter pieces.

Stay flexible and open to changing the original design if necessary. Continue attaching various items, and "take care to be spare." (Do not overdo it with too many fussy pieces.) Finally, add touches of paint if desired.

Protect the work with a UV-resistant varnish to prevent fading. Such projects can be free-standing or (if flat on the back) hung on a wall. Here is my finished *Escape from Exile*, about 7 by 7 by 16 inches tall.

Glossary

Abrade. To scratch or to wear, by rubbing with sandpaper, for instance.

Acid-free paper. Paper with a neutral pH. It is more permanent and less likely to become discolored.

Acrylic paint. A fast-drying plastic paint made by mixing pigment and acrylic binder with water. It is valuable for its permanence.

Archival. Made of acid-free materials that will remain stable over time.

Bleeding. The running or spreading of pigment through a layer of paint or water, usually (but not always) undesirable.

Bloom. A cloudy discoloration, or a wet-in-wet technique using bleeding.

Bond paper. Quality paper used for drawing.

Bone folder. A bookbinding tool made of genuine bone, useful for folding and creasing papers.

Brayer. A tool used to roll ink onto a surface by hand.

Charcoal. In stick form, compressed, burnt wood used for drawing. Also, charred twigs.

Collage. Papers and/or objects glued together in a pleasing composition.

Dry-brush. To apply relatively "dry" inks or paints lightly over a surface. A dragging stroke.

Faux finish. A fool-the-eye technique that mimics such visual textures as marble, granite, or wood.

Fixative. A thin varnish applied to a painting to protect the surface.

Frottage. Taking a rubbing of a textured surface.

Gesso. A toothy, plasterlike substance with a creamy consistency. Gesso is most often used as a ground to seal a surface before paint is applied.

Glaze. A thin, translucent or transparent coating applied over a painted surface.

Mask. An opaque shape or edge placed on a surface to cover and protect portions of it.

Matte. A dull, flat, non-glossy finish or surface.

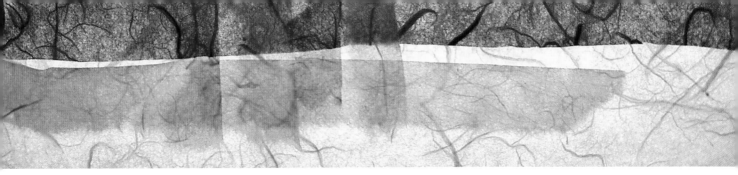

Medium. The material used by an artist to produce a work of art. Also, a liquid, paste, or gel added to or mixed with paint to alter or modify it.

Monoprint. A unique print. Sometimes one of a series, each print of which has differences.

Opaque. Describes something that cannot be seen through.

Palette. A slab of wood, glass, paper, ceramic, or plastic on which paint is laid out and mixed. Also, the range of colors an artist chooses for a painting.

Priming. Applying an undercoating to a surface as a base and to provide a seal between the surface and the paint. This creates a better bond.

Resist. A material used to preserve highlights or colors. Also, the method of preventing paint from coming into contact with an area or surface.

Sgraffito. The surface decorating technique of scratching through a layer of color with a sharp tool to expose another layer beneath.

Stencil. A flat object with a cut-out opening or holes. To stencil is to create a positive image by painting through the hole.

Tooth. The degree of roughness of the surface texture of a sheet of paper.

Translucent. Semi-transparent—describes something one can partially see through.

Varnish. A protective, transparent finish applied in a liquid state to the surface of a painting.

Vellum. Translucent art paper similar to parchment.

Wash. A thin, translucent layer of pigment that is applied to the painting surface, often with large, sweeping strokes.

Wet in wet. Painting in a new color before the previous one has dried.

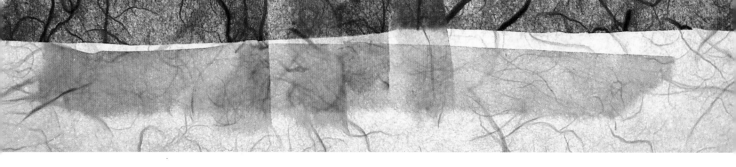

Supplies and Resources

Citra Solv, LLC
P.O. Box 2597
Danbury, CT 06813-2597
www.citra-solv.com

Colourcraft (C&A) Ltd.
Unit 5
555 Carlisle Street East
Sheffield, England
S4 8DT
www.colourcraft-ltd.com

DecoArt
P. O. Box 386
Stanford, KY 40484
Phone: 1-800-367-3047
www.decoart.com

Jacquard
Jacquard Products, Healdsburg, CA
Phone: 1-800-442-0455
See store locator page at
www.jacquardproducts.com

Pentel of America, Ltd.
4000 East Airport Drive, Ste. C
Ontario, CA 91761
www.pentelarts.com

Plaid Enterprises, Inc.
3225 Westech Dr.
Norcross, GA 30092
Phone: 1-800-842-4197
www.plaidonline.com

Ranger Industries, Inc.
15 Park Road
Tinton Falls, NJ 07724
Phone: 732-389-3535
www.rangerink.com

Sakura of America
www.sakuraofamerica.com

Tri-Art Manufacturing Inc.
www.tri-art.ca